NOTHING BUT
A PACK OF CARDS
A BOOK OF CARTOMANCY
AND TAROT SORCERY

NOTHING BUT A PACK OF CARDS
A BOOK OF CARTOMANCY AND TAROT SORCERY

S. Rune Emerson

Megalithica Books
Stafford England

Nothing But a Pack of Cards: A Book of Tarot Sorcery and
Cartomancy
by S. Rune Emerson
© 2016 First edition

Editor: Jennifer Linsky
Cover Art and Design: Storm Constantine
Layout: Taylor Ellwood/Storm Constantine

Set in Magna Veritas and Book Antiqua

MB0182
ISBN: 978-0-9932371-9-5

A Megalithica Books edition
An imprint of Immanion Press
info@immanion-press.com
http://www.immanion-press.com

ACKNOWLEDGEMENTS

To my mother, Misty Yeoman-Jones,
and to my sister, Lee-a Frasch,
who always knew I'd write a book:
thank you for believing in me,
and for teaching me what magic really was.

To my family:
Gregory Robertson
Michael Campbell
Nate Viner
Jeanne Trend

Without you guys, this book
would never have been begun,
let alone finished.

To all my friends in the community,
who kept insisting I write a book on this subject -
thanks for inspiring me.

TABLE OF CONTENTS

PREFACE

Writing this book has been a complicated experience. The art of magical images and talisman-crafting has been a longstanding interest of mine, dwarfed only by my interest in the arts of divination and magical information gathering. Thus, the book you hold in your hands now has been something of a dream (and not always a pleasant one) to write.

The subject of magic as a practice, especially in this modern age, can be tricky to write about. One of my favorite quotes about this comes from a modern television show, "Once Upon a Time." The character Jefferson states "You know what the issue is with this world? Everyone wants a magical solution to their problem, and everyone refuses to believe in magic. " [1] I think that's true - people who study magic often want to conflate it with the common philosophies of modern science or ancient religion, both of which offer up solutions to problems as if everything were easily explained in small bite-sized platitudes or theories.

Nowadays, science and religion do the same job. No matter what the interest is starting out, the finished product is designed to make people feel safe and secure, to help engender trust and faith. This can be dangerous, as it makes faith into something uniform instead of something personal. Concepts formerly offered as hope for a personal conflict become universal blanket statements of fact, despite the priests and scientists all being perfectly aware that we do not know the smallest bit about the universe.

Magic, on the other hand, is always personal. It says to us, "your wishes have strength, but they also have cost." It offers us a chance to achieve our greatest desire, if we are willing to pay the price - whether it be a personal sacrifice or loss, or simply a whole lot of time and practice, we won't know until we step off the cliff or walk away from it. And the price changes from person to person - it is never the same.

Magic reminds us that nothing is impossible, that there are no safeties or sureties or guarantees, and it removes the blindfold from our eyes. We are fools, and we dance on the cliff's edge every day. The world is not only dangerous, it's wondrous and full of experiences we never dreamed of. Reality eclipses our imagination's ability to conceive its outer limits.

And yet, somehow, our imagination and will have the ability to affect this vast mysterious universe and change it. I think that's probably the most miraculous part of it all - that it is so huge and mind-boggling, and yet such a small thing as a spell has the capacity to change its entire layout.

I suppose that's why I love tarot cards so much. A game designed sometime between the 11th and the 15th centuries, played as a trick-taking game, the alleged "devil's picture-book" was designed as an artistic metaphor for life; literally, it was a game about life. The occult aspects of the tarot are something of an amazing joke. Imagine if we took the board game known as the Game of Life and turned it into a system of magic and divination. That's exactly what happened, and I surmise it happened in no small part because of the reaction people had to that famous Dominican sermon, which castigated the "game of triumphs" as the devil's tool. [2]

The cards make the whole world into a game, reducing every person, place, object, or event into a two-dimensional pasteboard which (astonishingly enough) actually deepens those subjects and makes them more meaningful. Rather than diminishing the importance of life, it expands it in our minds, allowing us to see connections we never noticed before. I find that remarkable, to say the least.

This makes the tarot something unique as a magical tool. Nearly anything we can think of can be used for mystical purposes. From ordinary houseplants to a mother's advice, from clothing to toys, everything possesses a virtue and a mystery - and the word "occult" literally means "hidden or mysterious." However, there's a long stretch of difference between something which is useful for a spell or two, to a single object which can not only assist you in any spell, but can actually teach you any kind of magic a person might ever care to know.

When I was a child, I always wanted to find one of those "ancient grimoires" I always saw in television shows and read about in novels. You know the ones. Whether they were a checked-out library book or a huge leather-bound tome, they had everything in them. Spells, potions, rituals, lore - anything and everything was in those books. And we knew they were special, because the books often were depicted as being strangely magical, protected by spells or even maybe alive and aware.

I wanted a book like that, badly - probably more than anything else in the world, really.

Years later, someone told me that a tarot deck was an ancient book of spells and magical initiation, that it came out of Egypt and had mystical encoded knowledge in it. While I now know that "history" to be a fabrication, I can't help but be grateful for having heard it. It sparked something in my mind, and it let me look at the cards in a brand-new way. And, to be fair - while it may not have been true in the eighteenth century (when Antoine Court de Gebélin [3] published his spurious analysis of the so-called Book of Thoth), it can be said that it is true enough now - many tarot artists design their cards with the intent to teach mystical traditions and concepts through the images they create.

Later in life, I stumbled across some of the grimoires written by ancient medieval magicians - books like the Key of Solomon or the Picatrix, and was (perhaps unsurprisingly) disappointed. Small and dry, brittle in both page and concept, they weren't what I was hoping to find. I wanted a book that made the world alive and taught me new and amazing spells, something that was always relevant.

The Tarot is all of these things, and it is my hope that this book will help you, the reader, learn to work with your cards in the same manner as I have, and maybe come to love the cards as I do.

Within these pages, you will find spells and remedies, to be sure, but also the basics of sorcery in general, and the practice of card-based magic. As magic is personal and often subjective in pursuit (though objective in manifestation), I must make this disclaimer: your mileage may vary from charm to charm, from exercise to exercise. Learning magic requires one to trust one's journey and one's guide, and so I must operate under the idea that my readers trust me enough to make proper use of this book.

However, the theories within this book are as sound as I can make them, and if my suggestions do not aid you in learning, you may be able to innovate your own experiments and models simply by reading mine. After all, one must shuffle the cards to read with them properly; they aren't considered "wrong" or "out of order" when they are being used.

In any case, I hope this book (and your own pack of cards), guide your steps toward fulfilling your own wishes, as you make your way towards mastery of the Unseen.

S. Rune Emerson, cartomancer

CHAPTER ONE: THE PHILOSOPHY OF SORCERY

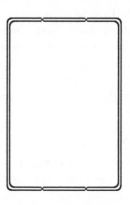

Of sorcery of any kind, one thing must be understood. The gross follows the subtle. It is not the Apparent forces of nature, the wind and lightning and the shaking of the earth, which are truly being manipulated. Rather, it is the Unseen forces and substances of reality which are moved. Sorcery is the art and science of true causation, not the topical changes of base matter. It is interacting on this level of existence that we begin to truly understand the nature of reality and thus the true work of the sorcerer. In our arena of Cartomancy, we begin our study with the observation of two concepts - Light and Darkness, and their two abiding qualities - that of being Apparent or Unseen.

Darkness is the word we use to refer to that which is substantial, the solid and manifest aspect of reality, that which is changed or acted upon. It is the fundament, the existence of all meaning and virtue, be it flesh or spirit. Darkness is the mother from which we have come, and of which we are still made - like stone shaped by an artist, like the blank page which becomes a poem only by the power of written word, so is Darkness. It is existence.

Light is the term which refers to that force which shapes the substance of the Dark - the artist's brush, the carver's chisel. It is that which brings creation or destruction, affording change and also affirmation or validation to the secret mystery hidden within the shrouded folds of something's being. A secret being known, the force of birth bringing forth a new life from the womb. Light is manifestation and exaltation, catastrophic obliteration and divine revelation.

The Unseen is the state of having yet to be shaped, the potential state which lurks within all things, when the Eye is not fixed upon them. Within the roiling chaos and fugue of the Unseen, deep forces move and create shapes, which just as quickly disappear, fleeting visions which fade in and out as if to lure one's perceptions, drawing one's Eye to seek, and by seeking somehow part the mists and conjure forth the Unseen into vision.

The Apparent is the state of things which are accepted and held by the Light of Vision. By this effort is ambiguity shaped into certainty, and accident crystalized into pattern. That which is, and has been, and cannot be undone; a safe haven to our souls, a sanctuary for our fragile psyches, possessing and invested with the nature of the chaotic forces which shape reality, but lacking their potency. Though the Apparent is fraught with cruelty and harshness, it is nevertheless a palace of safety for us, for it is constrained and limited, and therefore predictable.

And therein lies the power of Cartomancy, and sorcery in general. In order to work the magic of the Cards, one must learn first to predict with them, to sense the movement of the subtle and its Manifestations in the gross. And once one has done that, one can harness those subtle currents carefully, oh so carefully and bring forth the Manifestations one desires. Which, of course, is the nature of sorcery.

To sum up the basis of Cartomantic Sorcery, "the Light shapes the Darkness, in realms Apparent and Unseen." The concept of Light as a metaphor for mystical power and force is not new, but it must be understood to properly be used. The word "Light" is employed as a metaphor rather than a literal term - though psychic perceptions might in fact perceive "light" when witnessing magic, it is not an actual physical light which does the work, nor is there any sort of energy present upon the physical plane which can account for sorcery.

The word "Light" is used as a metaphor because of what it implies - light reveals, and what is illuminated is perceived.

Perception brings attention, and attention can bring change. Essentially, that which is illuminated is changed to suit the observer, through the very act of their observation, due to the nature of their method of perception.

What a sorcerer looks upon is illuminated by his Light. That Light changes the Darkness of a subject, in accordance with a sorcerer's vision. Light shapes the Darkness. That is, in a sense, the meaning of the lemniscate, the infinity symbol floating over the heads of both the Magician and the maiden in Strength, two figures in the Trumps of the Tarot. Light shapes Darkness, which makes way for more Light. Light into Darkness into Light; a continuous cycle.

Of course, there are more conduits of Light than just the sorcerer. These are called Mediums in our practice, and we will discuss them in more detail later. At the moment, however, it is important to know that there are four kinds of Medium one can find to conduct magical force (which we will simply refer to as Light from this point on):

Integral Mediums: Light reflected through an intrinsic and crucial quality within a subject; a mother's love, a cry of pain, a memory, a wish, a smile, the color of someone's hair. These Mediums are part of the subject, and possess a unique virtue, separate from the whole subject.

Fundamental Mediums: a subject which reflects Light just by virtue of its existence; the herb vervain, an ancestor's skull, a poem, the Eastern wind, a ley line under your house. These Mediums reflect Light as a whole, and their virtue is shared by utilizing the Medium entirely.

Transcendental Mediums: a conduit of Light which transcends mortal limitation and expresses itself through relationship rather than embodiment; the blessing of a goddess of love, the curse of a demon of greed, the will of the great Sea. These Mediums belong to forces which are not temporally limited, things which exist throughout time and space in multiple places (the goddess of love, for example, is present in all forms and acts of love everywhere). The Light comes from their relationship with the mortal world, primarily through pacts of patronage or allegiance, or through invocations and rites of apparition.

Ephemeral Mediums: transitory conduits, which go

beyond the limits of even the Transcendental; a moment of pure happiness, true love's kiss, a Solar Eclipse, the Winter Solstice. These Mediums conduct their Light through death and renewal. The moment of change and action releases their power.

A subject can obviously be multiple kinds of Mediums at once, and that is part of the Art of sorcery. Learning to work with and adapt Mediums to bring forth the right kind of Light for a situation is one of the major goals of mastery. A tarot card becomes all four of these Mediums rather easily, being simultaneously a beautiful piece of art (fundamental) with a specific meaning (integral) relating to a deep mystery of the universe (transcendental), appearing in a position in one's spread that it may never visit again (ephemeral).

This is why Tarot can be used for so many kinds of magic, not just divination. Each card is a Medium on multiple levels, and represents one of the many Manifestations of our reality, signifying a change or a subject of change in a way that puts the Light under our authority.

However, wielding the Light is not for the weak of will or the faint of heart. Magic exacts a cost from us as we use it. Those who Wander into the use of sorcery in ignorance often find that the more magic they wield, the more they have to wield in order to keep afloat. This can only go on so long before it eventually destroys the sorcerer (usually through one's own mortal frailties such as greed or fear or hope or ego).

All forms of magic have a method of testing the user, you see. When we say that Light shapes the Dark, it begins within our own reality and existence, our own Darkness, first of all. Whether one is a witch, a shaman, a bard, or a wizard, magic tests the magician. We are not gods. Our magic is as mortal as we are, as natural as the world we live in, and we have limitations upon what we are capable of. These limitations are not imposed upon us from outside; they are natural limitations to our Darkness-of-being, and based on very natural laws and concepts. For example, we have no power to turn the Light upon itself; it is infinite, and all things possess it. Therefore, we cannot affect the will directly with any of our spells. Emotion, thought, memory - those we can shape, for they are of the Darkness within all things. In any battle of Light against Light (such as a battle of wills) however, if all things are equal on both sides, the defender wins.

And to even get to this point, our natures must be weighed and measured and tested, and then tempered and forged in the fire of Sorcery which we have chosen.

Our trials will force us to learn discernment and Knowledge, to learn resolution and strong Will. We will be taught Courage in the face of fear, and we will learn to maintain Silence in the face of uncertainty, preserving the mystery of the Dark while shaping it with the Light, never wasting our Light in complaint or doubt.

We will discuss this further in a later chapter, as the Tarot explain these trials in greater detail. For now suffice to say, the ways of Sorcery are deceptively easy to learn and simple to maintain. It is our own nature which tests us as soon as we hold the Light in our hands and bid it. Magic exacts its price from us all.

The Manifestations of Reality

When we observe the world's forces as Light, and the substances of the world as Darkness, and then we observe that such Light and Darkness can be either Apparent or Unseen, we are able to view the blend of such things, allowing color and shape in the form of Manifestations, which in our Cartomancy refers to all the many things which come to be. From stones and grass and rivers, to thoughts and emotions, to people and moments in time, all these Manifestations are a combination of Darkness and Light, possessing both Unseen and Apparent qualities.

When studying Manifestations, it behooves us to examine the four most primal Manifestations of existence, for it is they which provide the alchemical key to our Sorcerer's Stone. By understanding these combinations of substance and state, we can create the living Gold of our ideal into existence.

Power: the Apparent Light of change, the released force of revelation upon earth. Power is present in all Manifestations, and is what permits those things in Creation to change each other. From the strength in a jaguar's jaws which can crush life from its prey, to the trembling might of a mountain's molten core unleashed, to the gentle power of a child's touch to move the heart. All which exists in the mortal world, and much of the immortal world as well, is invested deeply with Power. In Cartomancy, we represent these Manifestations through the suit of Wands, Clubs, or Staves.

Mystery: the secret virtue hidden and Unseen in the Darkness of existence. Like treasures waiting to be discovered, like the subtle eddies in a deep wellspring which bends the brave light breaching its depths, these twisting currents lurk beneath the surface of all reality, and are what bring meaning to our existence. After all, it is not what we have done and been and which stands revealed which holds wonder to the mind. It is that which is becoming which truly enthralls us. These Manifestations are seen in Cartomancy in the Cups, Hearts, or Chalices.

Necessity: that Darkness which stands revealed and Apparent, the implacable and unfathomable law which holds all in abeyance. Creation has found a balance, and it is ruthless; very little can flout the great equilibrium and balance that the entirety of the Manifested world has set into being. Necessity is the hard aspect of being which has its own laws; if Necessity is defied, existence suffers. From the law of gravity which binds not only our bodies to the land, but also affords us air to breathe to the simplest of imperatives within a biological system, the desire to feed and reproduce, Nature has her own philosophy, and her fairness is what allows the other forces to coexist in harmony. These Manifestations are found in the suit of Swords or Spades in Cartomancy.

Fate: the Unseen Light of possibility, the force which shapes that which has yet to take form. Seemingly fickle and capricious, this Manifestation is a subtle yet insistent and pervasive force. It does not command; it sets a trap and cajoles the inner spirit. It is a spider web of design and chance, a play of dominos knocked over by the fluttering of a butterfly's wings. It is elusive, and affects one on every level of one's existence across time. Its strength is no less for its subtlety; delicacy does not mean daintiness. Indeed, Fate is the shaper of the design, allowing for things to fall into place. Cartomantic tradition assigns the suit of Diamonds, Coins, or Pentacles to these Manifestations.

These four Manifestations blend and shape to create both that which is Mortal and touched by time, and that which is Immortal and ineffable. Sorcery deals with both, for it is the business of a sorcerer (as we have already stated) to bring desire into being.

Those Manifestations within the realm of the Mortal are touched by all four of these, possessing Mystery and Power in equal measure, in accordance with Necessity and subject to Fate. The Immortal, however, may be of any or no interaction with these four Manifestations, subject to their influence only when the Eye of Regard is placed upon them.

Sorcery is a matter of creating and shaping Manifestations to suit one's ends, and that is where we begin.

ThE LIShT WhICh ShAPES ThE DARKnESS

In the Middle East in the time of early astrology, magicians worked with a simple principle of four forms of change.

Flesh to Flesh - using the body of one Manifestation to change another body, such as poisons to kill a person

Flesh to Spirit - using the flesh of a Manifestation to change another Manifestation on a spiritual level, such as the imbibing of entheogenic drugs to create a change in the mind

Spirit to Spirit - the use of spiritual force from a Manifestation to change another spirit, such as the art of persuasion or fascination

Spirit to Flesh - the use of spiritual power to change the flesh, such as calling the power of the stars to enchant a talisman for wealth

These four understandings of magic led to the development of many different practices. Discovery and utilization of a perfect force of change for any given Manifestation, be it spirit or flesh, was a constant pursuit for the ancient magi. The term "al-iksir," or elixir in modern vernacular, represented a Manifestation which was able to transform anything it touched except itself. Finding the perfect elixir for a specific change, such as an elixir which transformed the body to health and youth, or the transformation of base metal into Gold

21

(the concept of gold being a metaphysical term for perfection as much as material wealth), represented the ages-long quest to which a great majority of magicians all over the globe committed themselves.

As we have discussed already, the tradition of Cartomantic Sorcery we are learning here is one which views these "elixirs" as a method of conducting Light (mystical force) to shape the Darkness (the world around us). This is similar to the idea of "trapped light" present in the concept of astrological talismans (such as those discussed within the medieval grimoire the Picatrix, which I mentioned in the Foreword), which relies upon the idea that every astrological aspect gives off a specific kind of light, which can be sealed into a lustrous object (such as a gemstone or an amulet of glass) and used as a subtle effect of change upon the world.

Talismans made in this fashion are Unseen even to magicians; unless we can see the effects or the source of change, we often cannot even sense the magic being done. It is as if the magic is not magic at all, but simply the natural way of things. I mention this so as to showcase the difference between Apparent Light of Power, and Unseen Light of Fate - the difference between a force which is obvious and detectable to those who can sense such things, and an effect that eludes even the most acute mystical senses.

Many magicians in modern practice enjoy employing magical practices known as "energy work," essentially arts of Power which manipulate the essential forces of Apparent Light to effect change directly. This magic might be employed to call upon spirits or "energies" of various kinds, to create wards and protective boundaries, to unleash forces of change, or to bind and control a subject, or even to claim such Light as one's own through invocation and theurgy.

However, these arts are not the only ways of magic. For example, using the cards for divination is an act which relies upon the Unseen Light of Fate, letting it play upon the images to show us the deeper patterns in the world. This cannot be detected by magicians quite so easily, for it is not an art of Apparent Light.

Likewise, the arts of Apparent Darkness such as healing or working the weather are detectable by those who are alert, but those hidden arts of glamour and enchantment which dwell in the Unseen Darkness cannot be measured by any but the subject; they rely upon a connection within shadows which can be used to cloud the inner recesses of the spirit. All of these magicks are the province of a sorcerer, not merely the unsubtle arts of "energy work."

Here we have a depiction of the world as seen through the eyes of the Arcana - the Sun as a symbol of the Apparent Light of Power and the Moon as a symbol of the Unseen Darkness of Mystery, which merge together into a vesica-piscis-style Eye. Within the sclera of the Eye we see Stars, representing the Unseen Light of Fate, which surround the iris of the Apparent Darkness of Necessity, wherein all of these greater essences are replicated and held in balance.

As a world model, this image offers three benefits for a cartomancer.

It affords an understanding of the four Manifestations and how they come about, and how the base versions of them we encounter in the mortal plane are reflections of their greater counterparts.

It also shows us that the forces work in harmony, which is

a guiding concept for any magician. Our circles reflect the Circle of Necessity, held in the dynamic juxtaposition of Fate between Power and Mystery.

This crossroads of forces is a natural place of balance, and magicians should maintain themselves in harmony with it, so as to keep equal parts of meaning and potency, freedom and purpose, within their Art. This balance reminds us that there are Laws which hold sway over even those who reconfigure reality's shape.

It allows us to see the importance of the Eye of regard - by our attention, so we reflect the attention of the great powers. Cultivating the Vision is a crucial art for a cartomancer, as where we Look, we reveal and shape. The paradigmatic elements of a sorcerer's magic rely upon a strong sense of rightness, a Vision that trumps any other it encounters, a true Seeing of the world which not only affirms the reality of now but also solidifies the road of the future. And that, of course, is what Cartomancy is all about in the first place.

We will speak more of magical circles and paradigms later in this chapter.

THE RULES OF SORCEROUS ART

The purpose of sorcery is transforming nature to fit one's desires. However, as we have discussed, nature is built of reflections and echoes of itself. This is no more perfectly apparent than in the simple understanding of the reflected nature of Apparent Reality and Subtle Reality, which are in themselves mirrors of the Light and Dark.

To manipulate Apparent Reality through sorcery, one must understand four basic rules, known as the Rules of Sorcerous Art. They are as follows:

The Triangle of Art - a sorcerer's magic is conducted properly to harness other Mediums by the combination of three inner qualities:

- A Will of Iron, unyielding and firm
- A Wish and vision, a clear and pure desire
- A leap of faith, a Surrendering to one's new reality, relinquishing the old

Smoke and Mirrors - the proper reflection of both the Light of change and the Dark substance of reality, Apparent and Unseen. This is accomplished by the use of sympathy, objects, and emblems which represent and adequately reflect the subjects and components of the spell.

The Alchemy of Naming - change in sorcery is accomplished through renaming and reification. One does not tell something what to do; one changes what it is, and then its actions will follow to suit its new nature.

The Pact of Power - all magic requires a power source, and sorcerers form Contracts with power, which they channel into their spells through the Mediums of their Paradigm.

A spell is a process by which a sorcerer calls upon a desired Manifestation. What a sorcerer Manifests is real, and comes into existence because it can and it must. These magicks are not lies or deception. They are true Manifestations; the only chicanery found in sorcery is that which is used to hide one's magical actions from those who might seek to sabotage them.

In particular, sorcerers are always attentive to three features of the Unseen, all of which may at one point come as confirmation of one's own spells:

Spirits, which are animated and intelligent reflections of a deeper reality of the Light, be it a primal power, an elemental force, or perhaps a memory of nature.

Signs, which are the umbral reflections of a stirring in the Dark, a coincidence or mysterious occurrence which can be brought about through magic or nature.

Visions, which are emanations of secret wisdom and gnostic inspiration filtering in from the Light and Dark into this world, names and lore of power from other places which teach us.

It is these forces which sorcerers use to bend reality. By utilizing a Vision about something, like its name or its secret paradox, a sorcerer can affect it. By calling upon the spirit of a force, they can wield the force by manipulating its reflection. By following the Signs of illness around a person, they can manipulate those forces which cast that omen, so that the person is healed of a disease.

It is thus that we practice our Art. Through shades and reflections of nature, sorcery redefines not only the being of a Manifestation, but also the relationships of its aspects to other Manifestations.

The Five Forms of Manifestation

The sorcerous arts are practiced through the use of five key Forms, also known as the Five Arts of Sorcery. These key Forms can be found as aspects in all Manifestations from thought, to person, to event. A sorcerer learns to work with these aspects as Mediums, and indeed the body of a sorcerer's spell book will be riddled with references to these aspects in one paradigmatic form or another.

Umbra: the Shadow of a Manifestation, often associated with the Trumps. A Manifestation's Umbra is its influence, the scope and breadth of its power to affect and hold those things around it. All of us have an Umbra - a reach and a tether to all things which are within our power. Like threads of power woven into a circle, we spread our own influence into the world through various means, marking each other and touching each other and placing our seductive elixir into each other's hearts and bodies. Benign and malefic at once, the Umbra is a measure of our hold upon our reality, and what Manifestations within it we can affect.

Imago: the Image of the Manifestation, affiliated with the Wands. Of particular interest to those of us involved in the sigillic arts of Cartomancy, the Imago is the shape of how a Manifestation presents itself. Not only a vision it presents in the current moment, this is also the design of the future as it shall be revealed. Imago is more than merely the shape of now; it is the destiny of the Manifestation, shaping itself line by curved line, shape by formed shape, to a greater design. Like the liquid remains of a caterpillar shaped into a butterfly by hidden design, so the Imago manifests the present into the design of tomorrow. When casting a spell, this Aspect controls the appearance of a spell.

Speculum: the Mirror of a Manifestation, aligned with the Cups. The Speculum is the mark of something's passing and existence, the channel linking the past to the present. All Manifestations leave a trail of their being. Like the Imago, this is representative of its being, but it is unlike the Imago in that it does not affect a change. It merely conducts and reflects. In spells, a Speculum creates sympathy towards a target.

Corpus: the Body of any Manifestation, represented by the Coins. Contrary to the gross understanding of this word, the Corpus of something needn't be physical. Some Manifestations may be purely mental constructs, such as a plan of action; others exist on a deep primal level embedded within the realm of emotion or desire or dream, or even encoded into something's Fate. The only defining factor of Corpus is that it is a complete encasing of the Manifestation, a manifest home within reality. It is the encapsulation of something's entire existence from beginning to end, possessing its conception and also its eventual demise.

Lingua: the Word of a Manifestation, denoted by the Swords. Not merely the word but the voice which speaks it, the Lingua is the message of any Manifestation, and how it chooses to define or inhibit subjects within its influence. In sorcery, we speak of the power of Naming - that a name is a binding upon that which is named, for good or ill. The Lingua of a spell is its boundary, for a Manifestation's Lingua is its identity and destiny, its own inborn necessity and drive to change its surroundings. From revelation to exaltation to destruction, this is the affirmed purpose and limit of Light within any Manifestation drawn out and etched upon reality.

Through the application of these principles, in accordance with the Rules of Sorcerous Art, we can begin to create our mystical practice and design spells that we can use for purposes practical and ambitious. The following example discerns the different aspects of a tarot card, and how each aspect aligns with one of the Five Arts of Sorcery.

Here we have the Two of Cups, representing love and union in most traditional readings. This card provides an excellent example for the Five Arts, which I will list below.

Perhaps the first place to start with this card is the Ars Speculum, because the card is a Cup, and the Cups denote avenues into the shadows of a person's Mystery and inner Darkness. The Cup in the card being held by the two figures already speaks of a shared pathway between their hearts - very appropriate considering the meaning of the card.

The Ars Imago of the card is of course the image itself, a gathering of symbols which evoke the feeling of love and union - two figures whose eyes meet over the icon of the Cup, which denotes Mystery (and not insignificantly the Speculum as we previously mentioned). Again, love and union are obvious from the image.

The Ars Corpus within the card lie in its use as an object of power itself. The card is itself a medium (as previously described on page 4), and can be used as a talisman in multiple ways.

However, Ars Lingua are present primarily in the borders of the card (which artistically limit the card's influence) and in the meaning of the card. Those who read with a tradition of meanings will see this card as affiliated with its meaning, using that motto as a baseline for any other interpretation.

Finally we have the card's Ars Umbra, which of course is most readily seen when the card falls into a spread, denoting its influence over the subject of the reading. Likewise, it carries its influence into any place it is carried, in spirit or in flesh. So too, it holds influence over any place where two hearts meet, for this card is the pathway between hearts.

In this manner are all sorceries made available to the Eye of the cartomancer. When working with the Two of Cups, one may utilize it for the opening of two hearts, or perhaps apply a different use, for example, communicating with a spirit whom one is connected to, or reinforcing understanding between friends.

The image on the Two of Cups advises us on ways to strengthen a spell for these purposes too, perhaps by including a chalice from which both people may drink, or by calling forth the spirit of the Cup to aid in understanding, or by simply finding a way for eyes to meet.

Indeed, the mirroring pose of the card implies that the use of a mirror could be applied for regarding someone via magic, which implies the worth of this card for scrying, a rather unconventional usage of a card that speaks of love (unless of course you're specifically peeking in on a loved one). Taking a look at the other Twos can further this perspective. For example, observe the Two of Wands seen below.

Holding a globe in his hand and staring out into the distance, the figure in the Two of Wands seems to also speak of seeing far (the literal meaning of the word "scry"). However, the implication in this card is one of seeing "far" rather than mutual reception in the Two of Cups. An important distinction, if one were to use it for changing someone's perspective, it implies a longer view, rather than an intimate and personal one.

Then of course we have the Two of Swords, pictured below.

Crossed swords, a blindfold - this conveys a very different message indeed. Sight is implied by the symbolism, but the message seems to be one of obstructing vision rather than aiding it. Considering that the Sword is the symbol of Ars Lingua, this card might create a limit to one's vision. Perhaps prevention of scrying is one of this card's potential uses? Carrying this card, or associating it with an object one wishes to cloak from divination might be an excellent use of Ars Corpus in conjunction with this card, while drawing a circle around an object using two swords might accomplish the same magic via the concept of Ars Umbra (especially if one uses a cloth to cover it).

The arts of Cartomantic Sorcery are actually quite versatile, as one can see. In our hands, the cards do more than read the movements of fate. Each card becomes an initiation into a spell or mystery of magic and their combinations expand into nigh-infinite possibility. The Five Arts, as simple as they may seem, contain an inclusive perspective of sorcery that allows for a great many magical workings. The only limit is that of our imagination and follow-through.

Now that we've covered the basics of sorcery, let us move into matters which demand our attention. From the Ars Lingua, we have learned that a limit is less a confinement and more a focus and a defining understanding, making magic actually more user-friendly. Now we shall examine the Nine Laws of Magic, which are the standards of Manifestation and harmony placed upon this world, as part of the natural way of things. Please remember that this is merely one of many paradigms of understanding; if this one doesn't work for you, there are other methods you can learn with just a little bit of research into magical laws.

The Nine Laws of Magic

If one would begin to learn sorcery, one should first start by understanding the basic principles of the Unseen and how it functions. Consider how one creates a deck of cartomancy; one takes the mad and random turns of the gross Apparent reality and ensnares it into a system of Cartomantic omens one can then turn around and read.

By Seeking with the inner Eye to see and understand the mechanisms and hidden laws which the subtle forces must heed, one thereby confines those forces to heed such laws. By observation, one coalesces reality. And thus, the first paradox of the sorcerer is born, for the paradigm of law is an imposed order, and will confine the sorcerer as much as his power.

But, that order must not confine too tightly, but rather be a true compact of understanding and respect and honor, demanding equal value from sorcerer and subtle force. For if the sorcerer's will cannot range true, no sorcery can be accomplished, and all is wasted. So too, if the forces cannot bend and move and surprise, their rigidity will be the downfall of the sorcerer.

And finally, those forces which the sorcerer harnesses through his magic must heed this balanced state, or they will defy the sorcerer, causing harm in response to insult. For such is the nature of magic - an offense and a theft, and a magician practices it because it is how we are Manifested to be, not because we wish ease or comfort.

Below is a list of the nine laws associated with the subtle forces which can be manipulated and experienced by the cartomancer. Observe them and with your Eye, unlock them from the shadows of the Unseen, and make them Apparent.

1. **All is One**: All things are one thing, in truth, merely components of one great vast organism. Any illusions of independent existence are merely phantasms of the ego. Magic is the communion of that One speaking to and redefining Itself, without dichotomy.

2. **As Above, So Below - As Within, So Without:** All things reflect what force they are borne from, what Manifestations and Forces they interact with, and what they remember. Indeed, there are three kinds of reflections which are absolutely perfect to a magician, and we shall go over them in greater detail later.

3. **Change is Constant**: Nothing is stable, and what is Apparent is changing at all times. Guiding change is what magic is all about; dramatic and flashy spells aside, it is the bending of nature's own inherent fluctuation that comprises the true purpose of the Art.

4. **Duality is Intrinsic**: Everything has its own indwelling polarity, equal parts front and back, Apparent and Unseen at once. Indeed, this is why magic is so effective. By calling upon a subject's own internal paradox, we can reduce its state and redefine its Manifestation.

5. **The Circle Closes**: Nature repeats herself in a never-ending chain of self-replicating themes. Recognizing these themes and learning to choose another theme to replace the current one is one of the secrets of magic. Each cycle is predictable, with an obvious start and finish, and so it will always be.

6. **Change Creates Consequence**: The rhythms of the Unseen are ruled by cause-and-effect within the Apparent, and all Manifestations can be either, for all is both, though only Apparently one at a time. If one's subject is a cause, one must transform them into an effect to neutralize them, and vice versa.

Also, there will always be aftereffects from any act of magic. Learning to measure the ripples of causation one creates is a constant challenge to magicians.

7. **All Is Born From Union**: This Manifest reality is built around and defined by the relationships between Apparent factors. Every act of magic, every knowledge gleaned, is a bond of union between the sorcerer and an agency of reality. It is these connections which create and redefine the world in the desired way, so a sorcerer should always strive to create unions with their actions.

8. **Everything Has A Price**: All changes exact a price from the creator. The price is in equal balance for the result. Losses bring gains, and so on. The greater the inner reality to be created from the Unseen, the greater the price within the Apparent.

9. **All is Sacred**: The subtle and the gross are ineffable, and indeed that which can be defined or reduced is immanent and divine; there is no evil, for true good has no opposite, containing all things. From Ordeal, to choice, to our purpose of being, this is the final truth.

Sorcery, as described earlier in this chapter, is performed through reflection and reification, with power conducted in accordance with design. Through the revealing of reflections and symbolic representations of change, and by relating such symbols to their relevant forces and substances in a sympathetic and irresistible way, we may move force by moving symbol.

This is the basis of the truest magic there is, the magic of Contract, the creation of symbolic and sympathetic relationships between two subjects.

In Cartomancy, this is most easily seen through the primary relationship of the sorcerer with his paradigm, the world of the Cards. The bond, and subsequent binding and releasing, of said magic is born of a contractual agreement. A force gives, and it gains. So does the magician. This is the core of all Cartomancy, and indeed it might even be said to be at the base of all magical practice everywhere.

In order to truly tap into this practice, a sorcerer must first learn what it is the Cards can offer. This is no simple task, but a test which will try all the powers and skills of the magician.

SELECTING A MEDIUM

One's second step as a magician is to define one's dedications and practices clearly, so that one may coax forth the powers immanent and hidden within the world. This is done in all sorcery by the selection of a personally significant Medium.

As mentioned before, a Medium is the channel and the material agent through which one conducts, fascinates, and measures the subtle forces of Light one touches. It is the conduit for the Power one wields. For a cartomancer, this begins with their deck of Cards, as simple a method as any.

Like all good reflections of nature, it defines and expounds upon the details accurately, and can be used to reach and embody any factor within the Apparent, and can provide vessels and focal points for the Unseen to act.

A Medium has the following aspects associated with it:

It reflects all of reality, Unseen and Apparent, in a manner like unto the shouting of one's true name or the sudden grasp of one's own face within a portrait. It defines in such a fashion as to captivate and enchant.

Inherent to its system, the Medium is fascinating and captivates the magician's attention, so as to deepen the connections of sorcery to their strongest level.

It describes not only the nature of reality, but also redefines the sorcerer in an empowered role, as the one who holds the power to change the world, separating all influences and conveying sovereignty unto the sorcerer by virtue of association.

It is a complete system, allowing equal parts predetermination and persuasion, affording equal ability to bind or loose the Unseen, fully immersive and interactive as a structure with reality at all times.

Some common Mediums have included magical diagrams such as the Qabala, key ingredients such as blood or mandrake root, certain sovereign spiritual forces such as demons or gods, and even icons of great potency such as the sword Excalibur or the binding cord.

These Mediums are the core of the paradigm of a sorcerer's Contract, and as such are representations of the sorcerer him- or herself, empowered and liberated. What is conveyed through these objects is conveyed through the sorcerer, and in later years they become interchangeable. As such, the Medium chosen holds certain counted burdens inherent to its nature, which must therefore be enacted and carried out by the wielder of the Medium.

The Paradigm

Indeed, there are as many Mediums as there are sorcerous paradigms with which to house them. From the Witch's Apple to the Wizard's Magic Circle, each Medium houses a vast potential of ability to re-present the world sorcerously. As this book will teach the reader, a cartomancer utilizes Cards as their Medium, each Card acting as a reflection of a singular Manifestation of the world in image form, describing pictographically every possible permutation of Creation.

If one would truly tap into the power of a Medium, however, one must first understand one's own paradigm and how it manifests. Most paradigms embrace one or more of the following four models, and Cartomancy is no different.

Animistic – a paradigm of spirits, life, sentient beings and entities of power

Energetic – a paradigm of forces, power, non-sentient states of being and relation

Psychological – a paradigm of archetypes, mentality, psychic states of consciousness and understanding

Memetic – a paradigm of intelligences, thoughts, cognitive processes and cosmic mentalities

Discovering which paradigms one's deck employs is the first step. A great many of the decks are psychological or animistic, as they feature personifications of forces through human figures and animals. This book, in fact, is written primarily in an animistic paradigm. However, some do not, and some also represent cosmic forces through non-sentient imagery, such as a mountainside or a wind or deep lake or swirl of stars. Some speak of energies, and hearken to eldritch or arcane systems of sodality and cosmogony, such as the Greek elemental system of Earth, Fire, Water, Wind, and the final Quintessence.

In some cases, however, the magician will wish to choose a deck based on a paradigm they wish to employ, rather than trying to learn a new paradigm through the Medium of a new deck. There is nothing wrong with this method. The skill of a cartomancer lies in wielding sorcery equally well through any system of Cartomancy, and indeed, the best deck for sorcery is one which embraces all four paradigms easily. As our purposes lie in learning all aspects of Cartomancy, this book will henceforth assume that you have managed to engage a deck on all four levels of paradigmatic interaction, and therefore are requiring instruction in all methods of use.

If you are having trouble figuring out which paradigm your deck of Cards is utilizing, a simple method of understanding can be in the way one defines oneself within the deck: the choosing of a Significator. Remember, all effective Mediums relate one directly to everything in the world, and empower the wielder to enact change.

The Significator

Quite possibly the very first magical act any practitioner of Cartomancy must learn is the choosing of a Significator, a Card which represents the subject being addressed by one's magic. To properly reflect and identify a target is the beginning of all magic, creating what we refer to as sympathy with the target of our spell. This may be a living person or animal, an inert or inanimate object, or even a location in space or moment in time.

In Cartomancy, a Significator can be chosen in three ways.

Traditional: One can use a system present within the paradigm of the deck, such as astrological references in the tarot, or perhaps elemental correspondences or numerological ones. This operates like a very firm naming or binding spell, allowing one to act upon the subject with impunity, by right of law and authority of reality itself.

Intuitive: One can use one's own intuition and inner guidance, drawing upon one's feelings about a subject and about a certain Card which corresponds well. This is usually most successful when working with a target one is well-acquainted with emotionally, as otherwise one can find that choosing the wrong Card allows the Cards an open channel not to the subject, but to oneself.

Serendipitous: One can use a random draw from the deck, face down, thus letting the Cards speak to the subject directly and offer a Card forth. This can be very useful when casting spells upon something one has no knowledge of; the random Card often operates as a divination first, allowing one to know more about the subject than one did, as payment for trusting the Card's powers.

Naturally, all of these methods of choosing are made more powerful by allowing the subject of the spell to choose its own Card. Should one find that impossible (for example in the case of enemies or those incapable of choosing), it would be best to be subtle about your choice and not let them know what you picked.

DRAWING THE MAGIC CIRCLE

The Paradigm of a magician is absolutely integral to any magical work, and any Medium a sorcerer works with must channel the power of that Paradigm clearly and well at the behest of the magician. In Cartomancy, as previously stated, the magician's Paradigm is made manifest through the Medium of their deck of Cards. This deck is in essence a magical circle, a boundary which draws the sorcerer's Umbra around all things in his or her life, as well as the Corpus of the sorcerer's knowledge, the Imago of the world being manifested, the Speculum of the past as the magician has experienced it, and the Lingua of transformative word which ensorcels the cartomancer's targets.

A sorcerer's magic works primarily through the magic of the Contract - something traded for something gained. As all things are shapings of Darkness by the power of Light, a sorcerer must ever be mindful of the shadowy and intemperate nature of the transient material world. As each Manifestation has moments of Apparent and Unseen Light and Darkness, flickering this way and that, the sorcerer must learn to acknowledge these shiftings and be unfazed by them, maintaining themselves in a state of perfect tranquility and balance.

To those of Asian bent, this is seen in the form of Earth qi; to the Western practitioners of Qabala, this is known as the state of Mildness. For a sorcerer, the magic begins when they are able to relinquish the obsession with the flavors of nature and embrace the fundamental state of utter balance, letting go of the aspirations of Lingua and Imago, releasing obsession with the Corpus and Specula of the world.

By releasing preconceptions and instead adopting a worldview that is observant without being obsessive, emotional without being unbalanced, they are able to take up the magic in its entirety.

When all forces are evenly matched, an exchange can be made, and that is the true magic of sorcery - the Contract. Within the Umbra, the Shadow of the sorcerer, all forces meet in equality. The Word is spoken over the Body; the Mirror projects the Image forward.

It is therefore the purpose of a sorcerer to spread their Umbra, their influence, everywhere they can without losing their state of balance. Since a sorcerer's design is to shape the world according to their vision, this is only accomplished by gaining influence over that which must be shaped.

A sorcerer must find ways to reflect the five Aspects of their Paradigm in their everyday life, drawing everything which interacts with them into their web of Art. A cartomancer does this by laying out their Cards in a pattern known as a Spread.

The Spreads of a cartomancer are not merely for divination; they are the intricate patterns which change the future, as each in and of itself is an Imago of a particular chosen

Manifestation. A Spread which draws the shape of a heart around a client's Card might be used to draw forth the powers of Love and Emotion, whereas a serpentine Spread brings forth the deeper mysteries of the snake, drawing out secrets like the venom from the fang of an asp.

In addition, a Spread can be used to call forth the forces inherent within a sorcerer's Paradigm. A Spread possessing a key Card for each aspect of Fate, Mystery, Necessity, and Power might be used as an excellent method of spellcasting as well as divination.

One might call upon the Light and Darkness in one's reading by seeing the inverted Cards as Dark and the upright ones as Light, with Apparent Cards being face up and face down Cards showing the Unseen. Indeed, remember that the Cards of a cartomancer are subject to no law but the cartomancer's authority and will; nothing says each and every Card must be turned face up.

Spreads of these nature will be discussed in later parts of the book. However, a Spread is not merely used for calling forth a spiritual force to be wielded. Spreads may also do the following:

Binding and consecration of new tools and regalia, which we will discuss in the next chapter of the book.

Protection of a subject or subjects, by keeping said within the environs of the Umbra of the Cards.

The concealment of a subject or subjects by the same means, through enveloping others within one's own Umbra of influence, and thereby enclosing them within one's own aura.

The crafting of a Contract between the magician and a subject, in order to fulfill his or her wish or desire, through the claiming of payment as witnessed by the spiritual forces of the cartomancer's Paradigm.

The charming and setting apart of a space, that it may be used more effectively for magic by the sorcerer.

The communion with other realities or spiritual entities, by making a between-place where they may be more easily understood and more directly experienced.

The warding away or breaking of spells by the pushing of one's own influence through the focus of one's Spread into another's spell.

The subtle bending of a situation to the will of the sorcerer, by drawing all present influences into the confines of the sorcerer's own circle of power.

These are just a few of the many examples to be found, many of which we will cover in some degree of detail within this book. However, it must be said - a magician alone, no matter how powerful, is still operating at a diminished capacity without the aid of spiritual influence. Thus, it is of paramount important for a sorcerer to employ her Cards to help her forge connections with the spirits or powers she will use to boost her magic.

In order to truly appreciate the weight of this magic, perhaps it would be wisest to further examine the practice of sorcery as a whole, and the reason behind the making of contractual agreements. After all, one cannot practice the Arte Magical without truly understanding the nature of magic.

The Binding of the Contract

In essence, sorcery is the causation of change through manipulating reflection and sympathy; this is something we have stated before. However, this is a very spare explanation, and it depicts a rather lonely existence. A sorcerer's magic has no stipulation upon it requiring the maintaining of connections with others - but a human's nature does. Being a magician can be very isolating, and isolation leads to madness for the human mind; many a sorcerer has been brought down by their loss of perspective and mental imbalance.

It should be known that a magician is a crossroads of spirits and strange forces, a person who is also a place. The primary Medium of a sorcerer's Paradigm is, in a way, a reflection of this - an image of the truth of magic, an expression of that ultimate moment of transformation and creative force, Light to move the Dark.

It behooves a magician, in order to maneuver these forces wisely and with clarity, to remain neutral in manner and demeanor, allowing such forces as are needed to pass through without hindrance. As we sorcerers are also feeling human beings with emotions and dreams and needs of our own, we must learn ways to become clear channels, Mediums in our own right for the forces we interact with. This is why we of this tradition call what we practice the magic of the Contract.

A Contract is, as previously intimated, a binding between two beings, one being the sorcerer, and one being the subject of magic. Through Lingua and Imago, the Corpus of the sorcerer and the ensorcelled are bound; the force of this magic is conducted through the Specula used within the Umbra of the sorcerer's Paradigm.

A Contract can come into existence in a variety of ways. If two beings give words of promise to each other, or if two beings compete for dominance, or if there is an exchange of feelings or dreams or wishes, all of these are Contracts. And, if they are witnessed by magic, they can become spells.

A spell is the unleashing of the clause of a Contract. Remember that relationships are what move the world. It therefore is important for a magician to make good on all Contracts they create, and to not incur debt caused by imbalance or overreaching. Their power will help them do this, if they serve it in return. In truth, all things are about exchange. Your body seeks to serve you with health and beauty, in exchange for good service in the shape of nutrition and proper exercise. Your mind is the same, and so are your friends and family, your lovers, your pets and belongings, and all things in nature. To be free of attachments and Contracts is a mystic's intention; to be free of debt and to serve these attachments in balance is the magician's.

Like Earth qi or the Pillar of Mildness, a magician must become an empty vessel for the forces of her or his life. A sorcerer seeks to call upon and wield the forces of nature. In order to do this, they must be receptive to such forces, in such a fashion that they do not become overbalanced and create harm.

A sorcerer therefore learns that the creed they must ever mind is personal responsibility; we have a duty to balance all our equations, taking payment when we serve others, and offering payment of equal kind in exchange for aid. After all, as the Eighth Law of Magic states, everything has a price. When a price is forsaken in one place, it will be claimed in another.

Before we go any further, I think it may serve us to discuss something of interesting in the practice of cartomantic sorcery: the concept of the Trick. In every magical tradition, they address something like this - special virtue to be found in objects or moments, unique powers within certain emotions, some form of quintessential substance, a "materia magica" if you will, ephemeral and found in all sorts of places, but not necessarily dependably.

Amongst cartomancers, this concept can be described through the term "Trick." A trick in card games is a finite amount of time wherein cards are played, after the duration of which has passed, the winner is declared. Taking a Trick is like winning a hand in a game - only in cartomantic sorcery, taking a Trick is taking a unique combination of Virtues from something or someone. In order to gain a Trick, one has to earn it, just like in a game. Generally, magicians gain Tricks as payment from a Contract, often paid by the spiritual forces marshaled around the beneficiary of our work. Sometimes this is deliberate, and sometimes it is something that the client doesn't understand per se. Either way, these kinds of Virtues must be earned, either by being offered up freely (symbolically or literally), or by winning it in some other manner. Contests or combats, for example, often constitute a form of Contract, as well as the kind of enmities that spring up between magicians and their rivals or foes.

A Trick can come in multiple forms - physical objects, a good day where everything works out, a change in one's life that one didn't particularly cast for (but still wished for nonetheless). Tricks are magic and wonder unbridled and uncontrolled, and they require focus in order to be used properly. Magicians earn Tricks through simply doing what they naturally do, which is one reason why a magician's life is often so isolating and strange. Common practices to help focus the flow of magic in one's life is to center, which means to bring your power back to its core and focus oneself on one particular purpose, committing everything to it. A sorcerer's method is to keep oneself focused on a wish, and let all powers move toward that Vision. Stating it regularly (through affirmation or dedication rituals) is a good way to keep oneself focused and balanced toward one's goal.

Often stated in conjunction with the concept of centering is grounding, which is often stated as "releasing energy back to where it came from." This is irrelevant to a cartomancer, as we focus power through our Medium rather than through our body alone, although we can channel through ourselves if we choose.

What's more important about the concept of grounding is the concept of the anchor, holding onto that which is the bedrock of reality. Nature magicians will root into the earth in their meditations, whereas singers anchor to the harmony of reality through listening to music and doing musical exercises. Cartomancers often will organize their cards or shuffle their decks to anchor to the movements of the Unseen and the Apparent, letting themselves realign to the Light and Darkness of the world.

In the Cartomancy depicted in this book, we do our magic through the use of basic rituals, and through certain regalia, related to the Tarot. Crucial regalia of magic include the Weapons of Sorcery, the Cards, and the Book of Magic. Other things may include ceremonial garb, special tools, and other such artifacts and accessories as would be handy. However, a sorcerer recognizes that by performing magic, they are creating a new relationship in the world, which must also be balanced so as not to create dangerous upheavals. We create Contracts in order to tilt, and then rebalance, the scales of Light and Dark, keeping all things stable within the greater pattern, and thus keeping wisdom in our work. A sorcerer must never overbalance, or misfortune will befall all involved.

The following is an exercise one can use to balance oneself, center and ground, and protect oneself mystically using one's Magic Circle.

CASTING THE MAGIC CIRCLE

Begin by sitting in a place where you can read cards. Lay a blanket out on the floor, sit upon your bed, sit in a chair with a table in front of you, whatever works for you. Many people prefer to face a particular direction when they do this; for example, the North or the East are common. Use your own judgment.

Take your cards into your hands, and begin to shuffle them, breathing in a deep and relaxed manner. Let all thoughts leave you, release all tension, focus only on the movement of the cards.

Hand over hand, shuffle and bridge, however you shuffle your cards, let yourself move in the rhythm of the cards. Some magicians prefer to chant while they shuffle, under their breath. For example, one could recite the four Powers of the Magus, or the Qabalistic Cross or the Lord's Prayer. Whatever serves you best, you may do.

As you do this, become mindful of what is happening on the Unseen level of things. If anything is coming into you from outside, like emotions you are sensing or perhaps noise disturbance, the shuffling of the cards stops it. If anything is coming out of you that you don't wish to go into the world, like your own emotions or magical power, the cards catch it and filter it.

You can feel around you that the shuffling of the cards is drawing a circle around you, a partition between you and everything else in the world. Anything which desires to approach you must first meet the cards, who are now guarding you. The cards will test them. The cards will turn them. The cards will ensure they are worthy of meeting you without throwing off your harmony. Let the world be released, until it is only you and your deck together, the center of the universe. This is centering.

When you feel this, you can stop shuffling.

Now you begin to flip the cards face up, one by one, and sort them into piles (not numerically, just into piles of random order) - Trumps into one pile, Wands into another, Swords into a pile, Cups as well, and Coins into a pile of their own. Card by card, each pile grows until all are distributed. Place the piles in front of you with the Trump pile in the center, the Pentacles to the right, the Cups to the left, the Swords at the top most, and the Wands closest to you. This is your Circle, with the Five Aspects and Arts all in balance, with the four Manifestations surrounding the magicks of Sorcery, the suit which represents you.

Touch each pile and name it - "Umbra, Imago, Speculum, Corpus, Lingua." Go in whatever order you prefer. You are affirming the foundation of your Art beneath you. This is grounding, and when you feel the bedrock of your magic beneath you, you are done.

Flip over the top card of each pile, and let each one become a ward, a power which stands between you and the world. It will give you a gift - for example, speed or strength or quickness of wit, or perhaps a fog of mystery over you. This is warding, which protects you from danger.

This exercise can be done daily, and usually in just a few minutes. It is excellent standard maintenance for any magician's cartomancy practice, and can also allow us to look forward into our day and prepare ourselves. One must always remember that one's magic begins with oneself, and never shy away from using one's sorcery or divinatory skills for one's own need. By remaining in harmony and consistent contact with our own powers, we keep our balance with the other forces and individuals in this world.

ON THE NATURE OF THE SOUL

Sorcery is, as we have stated again and again, a matter of balance. However, the balance is not found in material exchange. As a spell takes place in the subtle realm, so must the price exacted for the exchange come from that ephemeral place. This principle is what fuels the taking of Tricks.

Simple actions are easily balanced. What feeds the soul must be replaced by a piece of the soul. Wishes are the Dark begging for Light; it is the province of the magician to serve this in a way that does not draw the magician into debt. So, to bring Light to Dark, Light must be offered in payment.

This Light is known to most as a soul, an immaculate and

perfect immortal essence. However, a soul is not the thing people believe it is. All things have soul - emotions, memories, qualities, objects, relationships. Anything which brings forth Light to move the Dark possesses soul. Indeed, soul is Light from within.

Stingy and foolish magicians will try to husband such things and hide them from others, believing that souls are currency and power, for indeed they can be used in such a fashion. However, remember that a magician must never incur debt, for when one incurs debt, the state of one's own clarity as a Medium is unbalanced, and the debt creates a current of change in a person's light.

Fate and Necessity, Mystery, and even the Power of one's self and others may rise to rebalance the chaos, causing misfortune to befall the magician within her or his life.

The scales will always balance, and all prices will be paid. This is what mystics will term karma, among other things, although such words are inadequate to describe the true mechanism of Contractual Magic, and indeed they are often taken out of context.

To understand, think on this: all things reflect anything they have become acquainted with. Thus, what you do is reflected to your life. In most cases, this is an automatic; you touch water, you get wet, and so on. In other cases, such as magic, this is more subtle. As you have moved the Dark with Light, so you are moved through Dark by Light.

For this reason, a magician will act responsibly. We will own our mistakes and rectify the trouble we cause, and we will rarely aggress against another. We will only offer harm in payment for harm, and always with caution; it is not wise to act in unnecessary cruelty, as one incurs debt. We do not kill, unless we have to or it is the dictate of nature. We do not lie, for our words bend life's reflection. We do not steal, for we would have to bear a burden for that.

Finally, should we incur a burden for whatever reason, we seek to repay that debt. It matters not if we think the other being deserves it. All are deserving. It is nature.

All spells of a sorcerer are Contracts being woven or unleashed, as we said before. The calling of the spirits of one's Cards are one such contract. In order to call upon such power, one must teach it that you respect and honor its mystery, and initiate into its wisdom. Sometimes this is done through ordeal, sometimes through intuition or cleverness.

Whatever the proper price, the sorcerer must pay it, and only then will the Contract be sealed. To seal a Contract with a Card, a sorcerer formalizes this through a ritual within a sacred space, and the Card is accepted as payment, allowing the magician to gain access to its magic.

This is seen through the "Card-a-day" practice cartomancers often undergo when learning how a particular Card works: they draw a Card to foretell the day, and then they document their discovery at the end of the day, in their Book of Magic, perhaps adding a new Spread or spell to their Book as well.

The sacred space of a sorcerer, drawn as a Magic Circle around them by the icons and emblems of their Art and Paradigm, acts as the open eye of the Powers of Light and Dark, witnessing and enforcing the Contract sealed, binding all parties to agreement. Thereafter, the Contract is binding. This works upon the spirits of the Cards, just as it works upon any being. The exchange of soul is given, and the spell is done.

This is at the root of sorcery.

A NOTE ON HARM:

Remember - offer harm as payment, never as gift. You would not want the payment for such a gift. Likewise, be wary of greed or self-delusion; these incur debt, and are never easy to pay. For a person to subsist in their illusions requires a price to be paid, for the world is truth, and truth demands its due regardless of our feelings.

We shall examine the beginnings of the sorcerer in the next chapter - the donning and claiming of the Regalia.

CHAPTER TWO:
THE CARTOMANCER'S KIT

The Art of Sorcery is a profession, like medicine or sculpture or smithing. And, like any profession, it has its tools of the trade. The following chapter is about the kit of tools needed for the work of cartomantic sorcery, which fall under two categories: Weapons and Regalia.

THE WEAPONS OF SORCERY – THE LIGHT TO BIND THE DARK

The first things the magician needs to acquire upon beginning their studies as a sorcerer are their Weapons. The Weapons are symbolic representations of the Suits of the Tarot, and are used to claim the magic of the Five Arts of Sorcery, as seen through the myriad depictions of nature's primal Manifestations. However, these Weapons needn't be identical to the ones used in a Tarot deck; indeed, they must merely be capable vessels by which to channel the virtues of said Practices. In this chapter I shall explain the Weapons and their associations to various aspects of sorcery.

The chapter after this one will detail how to choose and consecrate one's Weapons, and also how to use them in addition to many other useful spells to be worked with the various Regalia. Please be aware - the elemental associations commonly seen in the Tarot are not only not referred to in this book, but are actively avoided. This is because the elemental associations are tied to specific traditions which are not the province of this book, and also because the author personally does not practice magic of the common tetra-elemental variety.

WEAPON: THE WAND

The Wand is the weapon which is bound directly to the Contract of the Paradigm itself. It is associated with the practice of Imago, the crafting of the Image. Where the Wand is wielded, the entire weight of the sorcerer's magic is unleashed. Whether it be to charm a protective space, or the casting of a binding circle for forming of a Contract between the sorcerer and another being, or even to wield a Contract already formed, the Wand is a key to bind or loose the Power of the sorcerer. A truly dedicated sorcerer should never be without his or her Wand. Therefore, it should have a few qualities:

The Wand should be portable, so that it can be taken places. It should not be unwieldy or too awkward or strange to carry around. If the Wand is elaborately decorated, this should be in a manner that is not un-useful for the magician to have at hand. Some Wands are quite small, although most have a presence or size large enough to be visibly wielded when used; a hand-span is usually the smallest.

The Wand should also be durable, so that it cannot be easily broken. If the Wand is broken, the Contracts are no longer easily wielded, and a new Wand should be acquired and sealed to the circle of one's Paradigm so that they may be used once more.

The Wand should also be decorative of both the purpose of the sorcerer, and also the nature of the sorcerer's bearing. Large decorative staves are all well and good, but a witch who uses the powers of the underworld would likely find little use in a golden Wand decorated with hearts and cherubs. So also, some Wands are not sticks, but are fine to use-- pendulums, keys, and fans are also common.

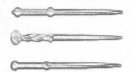

WEAPON: THE SWORD

As the Wand is a Power designed to command the Light manifest as a method to exalt, so the Sword is that same Light empowered to separate and conscribe, to bind and loose. Its primary purpose, associated with Lingua and Word, is for breaking spells and creating boundaries. However, it can even be used to obliterate a foe's Umbra, or free a spirit from bondage, or open a gateway between realms or souls. Its association with Necessity is reflective of a knight's banner; all sorcerers must be able to unravel what is bound in their world against their will, and so their Sword is called forth from the need of their sovereignty to be absolute. Their blade says "you are in my realm now; relinquish your power or be destroyed with it."

The standards for the Sword are as follows:

Like the Wand, it should also be portable, and should fit well into the hand of the wielder. The Sword's usefulness decreases when it is too awkward to carry it around.

The Sword should be very sturdy and battle-ready; decoration comes second to utility. The Sword is the sign of the invincibility of the sorcerer's will and authority, and it must be strong and lethal.

The wielder of the Sword should practice and learn well the use of their weapon. This is not a toy; it should be treated with respect and care. Like the Wand, it needn't be a physical blade. Paper talismans, lacquered nails, even smoke from burning herbs such as cigarettes have been used to this purpose.

WEAPON: THE GRAIL

A vessel of Mystery, the Grail is the sign of the elixir. It is the holder of potency which invites others to accept it. Its purpose is to deliver spells to those whom you would ensorcel. From healing draught to love charm, the Grail is the gift-wrapping of your spell, the secretive and fascinating agent of delivery you utilize in your magic when you need to cast a spell with subtlety. Linked to Speculum, the Grail is effectively the gateway through which magic enters another Manifestation.

The Grail must have three aspects to it:

It must fascinate your targets and draw them into your Umbra, tempting them and making them lower their guard.

It must be versatile and neutral of aspect, so as to be useful for carrying blessing or bane as you require. The shape of a cup is unnecessary as a spell can be conveyed through food, through a mirror, or even through the application of a perfume as easily as through beverage.

It must give no hint of its purpose; whether kind or cruel, magic is mysterious and can only be understood through experience.

WEAPON: THE COIN

The Coin is the token of a sorcerer's art, the method by which a sorcerer uses his or her magic to offer up payment for a change. Linked to Fate, these objects represent a marker of destiny, signifying a bond of promise from the sorcerer. The promise may be fulfilled as soon as the marker is given, or it may stand in wait as a recognition of debt (one of the special ways a sorcerer avoids debt by acknowledging it through an oath for the future). Although these tokens needn't be real coins, they function similarly to such mortal currency, but on a spiritual level. They represent the Corpus of the sorcerer's magic, usually something precious being given to the recipient, such as a day of good health or luck.

Choosing a form for your Coin is simple if you follow these three guidelines:

The Coin should be representative of the sorcerer's power in some way. The item chosen might depict an animal or other kind of totem special to the magician, or perhaps has the magician's name or special mark upon it.

It should be readily replaceable and easily acquired as an object of offering, as a sorcerer's Coin is the preferred method of payment to the spirit realm, and the occasions are many for a magician's need to have tokens on hand.

The objects chosen to stand as the Coin must be objects of value to the magician. If the sorcerer chooses to use silver acorns, for example, or perhaps a small wooden heart, the object must be of striking and singular appearance, easily fascinating those who receive them.

These Weapons are wielded as acts of destruction and creation; they are called Weapons for a reason. These four tools, and their symbolic representations, are the four cornerstones upon which one's citadel of magic is raised. Each represents a different aspect of the deep philosophy and law of the cartomancer's paradigm.

Indeed, learning to harness these four Weapons in more versatile ways is part of the Art of sorcery in the first place. A truly versatile sorcerer will initiate themselves into the mysteries of the Weapons, learning how to see all Images as Wands, all delineating Words as Swords, all inviting Mirror pathways as Grails, and all Bodies of virtue as Coins of Arte. They may adapt gestures of the hand or body, or perhaps incantations or liturgy, to represent each Weapon in a myriad of ways: spells to defend, spells to facilitate, spells to destroy.

The Weapons themselves comprise the first tier of mystical knowledge. Learning to work with them is the very beginning of cartomantic sorcery, for it is only with their aid that one can enter and gain the might of the further planes of our Art.

ThE REꟾALIA OF SORCERᴪ – ThE DARK TO AIꟾ ThE LIꟾhT

The following tools, known as Regalia, are each emblems of the magician's Umbra, their personal influence and sphere of authority. Each of these tools should be chosen with that in mind.

ThE FASTNESS

The Fastness is the altar a cartomancer carries with them - whether the Cloth and bag wrapped around their Cards, or the box used for storing all the Regalia, the Fastness acts as a protective and sacred space of opening for the magical work of Cartomancy. Chief among the tools of the Fastness is the Cloth; more than merely a clean space, the Cloth is the Umbra of a magician's sorcery. Laying the Cards upon the Cloth in a Spread is the same as casting a spell.

The purpose of the Fastness is to create a sanctuary of power around the tools known as the Regalia, which are the objects of sorcery which have less Weapon-like qualities. Thinking of them as the building blocks of the magician's haven, the solid manifestation of the Magic Circle, would not be amiss.

Other common tools chosen to be included as part of the Fastness include bags or pouches, boxes, flat boards for laying Spreads, and other such accoutrement.

Choosing one's Fastness (especially the Cloth) requires very little in the way of confining tradition, although there are a few hints one may use:

The Cloth should be large enough to perform one's largest Spread upon, and should not trouble the Cards laid upon it in any way. It is, after all, intended for use as a Cartomantic reading and working tool.

Each tool of the Fastness should be chosen for its concurrence with the tradition of the sorcerer. The design and colors should be geared around subtly reinforcing the magic of the Cards themselves, never so loud as to drown out the Spread, and never clashing with the fundamental practices of one's Paradigm and spiritual beliefs.

The make of the Fastness should be durable as well. Whether laying the Cloth upon the grass covered forest floor, or using a table in a sitting room, the Fastness should be well suited to handle any situation and should offer protection to one's deck of Cards. Indeed, there are no hard and fast rules on what constitutes a Fastness; one needn't even include a cloth, as a folding board will do just as nicely in many cases. In fact, some use a piece of their own clothing as a Cloth, lending a literal piece of their Shadow to their work.

Often included into the practice of the Fastness is the Garb, the clothing or gear a cartomancer wears as part of their work. Some tie scarves upon their heads for ceremonial reasons (and untie them in a reading for equally ceremonial reasons), others wear certain cords or robes, or perhaps necklaces or rings to provide specific resonances with the harmonies they seek to divine. All of these practices are designed around casting the Circle of their Art around their space, so they act as a sort of mobile aspect of Fastness, so that their space travels with them.

THE BOOK -
THE SHRINE OF SORCERY

No magician would be without their Book of magic. A magician's Book is one she or he writes for themselves; while many books may be used to expand one's learning, a magician's magic comes from the Light of their own soul. Any sorcery learned in the practice of magic will be linked to that Light, and so a sorcerer will carefully write down the shadows that Light creates, so as to better understand their own true self.

Within one's Book can be found spells and sorceries, but also meandering thoughts and ideas, theories and important memories. A Book is as much a journal as anything else.

However, a sorcerer who works with Cartomancy will also keep one very important thing in mind - the Book is the place of safety for the lore of the Cards. A Book of cartomantic sorcery will always be the final home of the magicks of the Cards, and indeed, some magicians keep their Cards within a book, or keep their writings in a box with the Cards. This is because the Cards are one with a cartomancer's magic. They share special space with the sorcerer's private thoughts, and they hold a unique and precious relationship with him or her. This is part of the Contract one makes with their deck; they will be treasured and loved, as they love and serve the magician well.

Tips to consider are thus:

Keep your Cards in or with your Book at all times, when not in use; they will serve you all the better for that trust.

Lock your Book. Never allow anyone to read the shadows or secrets you have recorded.

Let your Book have a Guardian spirit of its own, a Familiar spirit with its own sigil and identity, separate from the spirits of the Cards. A suitable Guardian can be called from any of the spiritual forces, although a force of Light is best forwarding the spirits which are housed and formed of the Dark.

More upon the Book and summoning a Guardian later; suffice to say that the Book is a special tool which will prove invaluable to any sorcerer. Remember to use it. Write everything down, and read from the Book regularly, and you will find some surprising insight. Much wisdom can be gained from reading one's own words after time has passed.

The Cards –
The Windows of The Spirits

Cards are naturally at the root of Cartomantic sorcery - no cartomancer would be complete without their Cards and their associated spirits. One usually acquires one's deck before one even seeks the other artifacts of the Regalia. However, if one has not done this, one should immediately proceed to acquiring a deck of Tarot Cards as soon as one acquires one's Weapons.

If one does not work well with the Tarot, one can of course utilize other oracle or divination decks. However, the Tarot are the tradition we use as a model for working with one's sorcery in this book. Each of the 78 spirits of the Cards, from the 16 face Cards of the Court, to the 40 Pips, to the 22 Greater Trumps, is a combination of all Five Arts at once - the Lingua of their chosen Name and Word, the pictorial Imago of the combined art of the picture with the various Specula of each individual symbol, and the Umbra found in the boundary of the card border, comprising the entire hermetic Corpus of an individual Manifestation. The deck is the foundation of one's magic - both its learning, and its doing.

The important thing to note about your Cards is that they, as an entire Medium (the deck) comprised of many individual Mediums (the cards, the symbols, the numbers, etc.) are your companion and your guide through your studies. The deck must therefore be something you resonate strongly with, something that fits your Paradigm and can adequately draw your Magic Circle around you.

Common ways to grow in connection with one's deck include (but are not limited to):

Sleeping with it beneath one's pillow (or next to one's head) at night. The added benefit of this exercise is that one may begin to have dreams pertinent to the deck's magic.

Keeping them with you at all times - carrying them in a pocket, purse, or satchel is the best method.

Pulling cards as a conversation, asking for their commentary on situations you are observing. For example, if you see two people arguing, ask the cards what they have to say about that argument. Their answers will help you develop an understanding of its personality and nature.

Shuffling and sorting your cards - it may not seem like a very big deal, but it's very important to learn how to handle and be familiar with your deck, both as a reader and as a sorcerer.

Keeping a journal of the cards and what they mean (this can be part of your Book as mentioned previously).

Eventually, a magician will learn to craft talismanic charms based upon the wisdom learned from their Cards, inscribing sigils and signs and pictures they find familiar from their deck upon stones and other curios, including the creation of paper talismans appropriately known to us as Card-charms. These charms allow a cartomancer to work with the magic of their deck of Cards through the creation of a reflection of a Card, thereby providing a window of its magic outside the deck.

Should you wish to craft a Card-charm for something talismanic or protective without giving away your own Cards, use these tips to do so.

Select an appropriate Card from your deck, through either intuition, tradition (tables can be found at the back of this book), or by random draw. Select also a material Medium for your Card-charm; paper is always appropriate, including card stock, although wood will also do.

Draw the sign and symbol of the back of your Card deck upon the back of the Card-charm first. This can be done with any pen, although you should seal it to your magical practice through your Weapons as a Sword or Wand first.

Use the same pen to draw the relevant signs of the Card chosen upon the new Card-charm, and also its name. The sigils should create a pictorial scene upon the Card-charm, and the name goes upon the bottom. You may also seal it by writing your own sigil or seal upon the charm.

Once these things are done, the Card-charm is finished, and may be used as a talisman to call forth the spirit of that Card for a variety of purposes, which we will study further in the next chapter. However, be minded of the following warnings when working with Card-spirits.

A Card-spirit needs limitations. Never unleash it to do its own will, for it has no natural understanding of healthy boundaries, and will do its elemental worst unless confined properly. Remember to give it proper instructions, including when to quit and sleep again.

A Card-charm should be burned or reclaimed by the Book immediately after it has done its job. Card-charms which remain at large after their work is done will cause havoc and chaos; spirits who lack a Corpus with the appropriate coping skills built in may become lost or insane. The Card-charm is a special spell, and should be used responsibly.

Only one of any specific Card-charm should be used at any time for any purpose. To do otherwise is to risk stretching one's Contract to the point of breaking. If you overtax your spirits, they will become worn and tired, and this is not minding the Contract of love and care you swear with them. They may be immortal, but they are not invincible and infallible. These spirits are to be used by you, not others, and any spells needed by people should be cast by you and paid for accordingly. Call upon your spirits to aid you in magic, but let the magic be yours and not only that of the spirits, especially when helping others.

A Card-charm can be used for a great many things. It can stand as a physical Medium for practically any kind of spell. It can be crafted to act as a beacon for the Card-spirit it is based on. It can even be used as a focus for a spell with multiple release points, such as a spell of Fastness or a trap spell.

The Fascinator

A Fascinator is something all magicians can make good use of. Mirrors, bowls of still water, crystal balls, and other objects of reflective quality are excellent for a great many magicks. They symbolize and represent the force of Mystery, and the ability to track the motions of the Dark when it is hidden from view. A Fascinator, however, is even more important to a cartomancer, as those who work Cartomancy work in close connection with that which is Unseen.

To a cartomancer, a Fascinator provides not only an excellent scrying device, used for spying magically upon the hidden forces and currents of Mystery, but also a potent weapon for sorcery upon others, and a tool for communing and housing spirits for easier communication. Common examples of

Fascinators include pendants and rings with large lustrous gems set in them, mirrors or glass beads, crystal sun-catcher prisms such as those hung on chandeliers, and so on.

To craft a Fascinator out of a standard mirror, simply inscribe your personal sigil and the emblem from the back of your Card deck upon the inner surface of the glass where it will not be seen. For other kinds of Fascinators, create a paper-and-ink version of your sigil, and burn it to ash, then mix the ashes with water and any oils you might wish to use, with which you shall anoint the artifact in question.

A very simple way to craft such a tool is to create a black mirror: acquire a picture frame, take the glass out, and paint it black on the side of the glass that faces inside the frame. Then, paint the aforementioned sigils on the black side of the glass when it has dried, and finally slide the glass back into place when all paint is dry. Your black mirror is the perfect charm for a great many magical workings.

Sample uses include the following:

Trapping a spirit who is dangerous, so that it cannot hurt others. This can be done by summoning it into your Umbra, which you can do by tempting it to manifest, then using your Wand to compel it into the mirror. The sigils you have painted within the mirror will bind it inside, until you break the glass or set it free with your Sword.

Capturing pieces of a person's soul without having them touch your deck. In this case, the term "fascinate" is literal: you must catch their attention with the Fascinator, and then while they are fixated, quickly cover the object and hide it away, taking their power with it.

"Fixing" an Image or spell so that it will constantly radiate outward from the Fascinator like a talisman. This can be accomplished by "drawing" the Light of a Card into the object via reflection of its Image in the Fascinator, then concealing the object as stated before. Wear the Fascinator or carry it to convey its presence into the world; the spell will be broken when the trapped image beholds its source Card once again.

Note that all mirror-charms used in these fashions will need to be cleansed with clean water before they are ready to be used again after such a use.

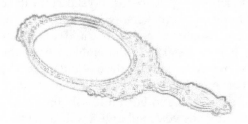

ᚠĦe ᚠᴀLKINᎶ Ħeᴧᑯ

A sorcerer can never be too careful, and will always need Light for her rituals. However, the Light a sorcerer wields is not the kind which is physical. Rather, we require illumination of the esoteric kind - for example, the Light of Truth (always needed) or the Light of the wisdom of a spirit on occasion. For these occasions, the true lamp of a cartomancer is also known as the Talking Head.

A cartomancer's Talking Head is a beacon, a vessel, and an amulet for protection against that which would harm or disturb us in our work. Usually either a light source (such as a lamp or candle), or a circular object such as a crystal orb or a skull (hence the name "talking head"), it provides sanctuary and conduit for spirits we work with, channeling their intelligence and aid into our space (and thus our cartomancy).

The Talking Head has four different kinds of Light it needs to shed, and often sorcerers acquire four candles, or a candelabra which can hold multiple flames, or an oil lamp with four wicks or some such, to denote these different Lights (although of course this is not necessary). Each of these four kinds of Light is unique and needed. These four Lights are (in our terminology) called:

The Light of Dawning Truth - to guide her in her sorcery and help her know her way.

The Light of Noontide Aid - to fortify and empower the sorcerer, drawing power to the ritual space and feeding it to the sorcerer.

The Light of Dusk's Cloak - to conceal the sorcerer and

make it so that what she does is never discovered.

The Un-Light of Midnight - to thwart all magic from other sorcerers, and prevent any tampering or attack.

It is important to note that the Talking Head is usually a treasured artifact of the shadow-casting sorcerer. Without it, they cannot perform much of the more subtle work of sorcery. The Art often requires a sorcerer to work at night, or to do things which others must not discover. We work in whispers and shadows, speaking to and working with spirits and otherworldly beings, seeking the signs and visions of the ethereal world. We move the Dark with the Light, and that means we must walk in both, but never solely in one or the other. The Head helps us do that.

To dedicate a Talking Head, simply speak a small spell as you light or place it. Any properly symbolic object will do, although most sorcerers prefer to use the same special Head for their magic.

The spell you speak should resemble this incantation:

Dawn for guidance,
Noon for strength,
Dusk for secrecy,
And Night Take the Rest.

Using a Head in your rituals will increase their strength and clarity, making it easier for you to focus your efforts, and drawing power like a beacon.

Collecting the tools of the Regalia, as with the Weapons, is a journey of self-discovery. It can be argued that this act is the very first beginning work of sorcery, that gathering the tools of one's art is a sort of invitation to the Light to begin revealing itself. Certainly there are a great many sources in this world which state that picking up and using a deck of tarot or oracle cards is tantamount to opening the door to what is often deemed "the Devil."

For a sorcerer, the taking up of the tools is an act of decision and affirmation, a choice to step into the shadows and wield the Light and Dark. This action begins a transformation of the self, an awakening and a reification of oneself as a sorcerer. That is the real place of beginning; when one identifies as a sorcerer, and allows oneself to become without getting in one's way, one enters the way of sorcery truly.

Make no mistake - the tools one chooses have their own magic, and in fact that is why they are chosen. They will take on a life of their own as they awaken to their path, much as we grow in strength and our nature changes as we allow ourselves to become a conduit of power, a Medium, in and of ourselves.

That being said, the Weapons are only weapons if they are wielded; the Regalia are only regal when they are worn in state. Any object can become a Weapon of Arte in the hands of a sorcerer, and the power to influence the subtle forces is not given to us through the tools, but rather focused and honed through our use of them. In short, a sorcerer's tools are knickknacks without the gift of a sorcerer to wield them. The cards do not lay themselves, nor do they read themselves.

We are the final tool in our kit, and we must allow ourselves to be so. We must allow that which we touch to transform and become exalted by magic, or the Grail we wield will be nothing but an empty vessel, the Coins objects of pale esteem. Our Sword shall have no edge, our Wand no authority to paint the world with Light. The Light is brought forth from everywhere, by us, and the tools we use are precious both for their own nature and for how they inspire us.

If your paradigm shifts and a tool is no longer a valuable Medium for your practice, replace it with all the honor you accord your own soul, for each artifact of a sorcerer is a vessel of our own Virtue, even if the tool wields no Light for us anymore.

Replace each treasured artifact of your kit willingly and happily, and with joy. Pass the tools along, or retire them to your collection, when you have moved beyond their wisdom. They are not useless because you do not resonate, and their destiny is only beginning.

CHAPTER THREE:
TAKING UP THE ART

The following section is a collection of rituals performed to harness the Weapons and Regalia of one's Cards, and to put our foot firmly upon the Path of Sorcerous Initiation. Sorcery as an Art is, as we've mentioned previously, deceptively easy. Mastering sorcery is less about power and more about finesse, and learning to use the tools effectively is a way to gain that finesse.

In this chapter, we will study various spells and charms one can use to work the magicks of Cartomancy. However, please understand that a spell is a process, not a staid and unyielding thing. These methods are tried and proven, but they are merely processes. The truest spells are the ones you design and test yourself.

Before we begin, a few basic steps must be followed when doing any spell. The following guidelines are designed to help a sorcerer perform any spell easily and well - indeed, if one cannot use these tips to cast a spell, then the spell should be adjusted. In times of old, these sorts of steps were often omitted from a text on magic, so that those who had not been initiated into the secrets of the magi could not perform the rites and spells within the pages of the book. This was one of many ways sorcerers and other magicians would protect the secrets of their Craft.

Step 1: Trust - While magic requires no belief in order to exist, a magician must believe in herself in order to perform admirably, just as any skilled person requires confidence to perform well. A magician must relax, trust in herself, and let go of belief, hope, fear, or doubt. Remember what you know and have learned, set your will, be brave, and be discreet. These are your first steps as a sorcerer.

Step 2: Relate - In order for magic to be done, a bond and relationship must form. Remember that relationships are what move the world. A magician must relate to the subject of the spell, and the ingredients and sources of power, and also to the relevant factors at work. In order to shape the Dark with your Light, be willing to get your hands dirty - mind the Dark's shapes and substance, and the forces you bend.

Step 3: Fascinate - A charm or a spell is an act of magic; all parts of it are hypnotic and entrancing. A sorcerer's power is their irresistible ability to fascinate themselves and the subjects of their attention. Chanting, eye contact, breathing rhythmically, hypnotic motion - these things can and must be used to draw yourself and your target into your spell; these are the part of the spell that people consider interesting. And remember, a spell affects you as well as your target.

Step 4: Assert - Sorcery is the practice of causing irresistible change through reflection. Make sure that all your actions are firm, sure, and descriptive. Tell the story, and make the story true; we do not beg or ask or hope when casting sorcery. We make our will happen, and when it's done, we acknowledge that it is done.

Remember, from this point forth, the exercises and work we perform is designed as an initiatory journey, each step taking us further and further into the practice of cartomancy, but also into self-discovery. It would be wise to log the developments one makes during this time, noting one's feelings and revelations as one begins to enter the world of the Cards. The experiences one has during this time will prove invaluable later, when one has time for reflection.

The Rite of the Adytum

To truly begin one's journey, one must first align the Weapons you will be using to the work of your Sorcery. The following information details a Rite which will assist in doing so, as well as various incantations used to harness the magic of the Weapons and Regalia this ritual will bind within. Think of this as your dedication ritual upon the roads of Sorcery.

Preliminary Exercise: Creating the Circle of Art

Before you begin working with your Weapons, you must first design and create a symbol of the Umbra of your own practice -

the Circle of Art. The Circle is a very personal symbol, but if you cannot think of one yourself, feel free to use any of the following Circles as templates:

Each of these templates is symbolic of a different aspect of the Rite we shall be doing. The first (on the left) is designed around a pentacle, each point of which denotes one of the Five Practices. Within the pentacle is a triangle with a circled cross, symbolizing the Triangle of Art, and the four kinds of Mediums. This is a very simple and focused sorcerer's circle, lacking unnecessary embellishment.

The second Circle we see has a cruciform in the center, a hexagram around it, and four eyes bound within the doubled frame of the Circle. This is symbolic of the Adytum, which is echoed in the card spread used in the Rite we are about to perform. It speaks of magic as a more theurgic and celebratory practice; each of the aspects of this Circle refer to a combination of Trumps we will learn about later.

The third Circle is a pentagram encapsulated by a seven-pointed heptagon, surrounded by a heptagram which is again bound by another heptagon, and then a seven-times-divided double circle surrounds the entire symbol. This is an echo of the Sigillum Dei Aemeth, which is an amuletic circle invented by John Dee, well known for his workings with angels and the Enochian aethers (also an "invention" of his). This circle is primarily designed as a ward, with each of the seven points operating as a protection, often tied to a name of power. The central pentagram (also called a pentangle) is again descriptive of the Five Practices, although Master Dee saw that as being more symbolic of the five aethers of his tradition, and the name of God.

In any case, we can see the basic formulae commonly used to design magic circles, which we will expand upon in a moment. For now it is enough to know how to start designing one's Circle.

We begin by drawing the Circle itself. Start with two concentric rings as a border, one drawn clockwise, the other drawn counter-clockwise, to represent the dual movement of Apparent and Unseen Light. Then, the inner pattern - this is usually a geometric frame or other form of lattice-work used to create the various vectors of the Circle. Finally, fill the Circle with symbols representing your own nature and the nature of reality, which symbolize the Apparent Darkness of being (the blank spaces in the circle act as signs of Unseen Darkness).

When designing a Magic Circle, the following guidelines may prove helpful:

Magic Circles are your tradition in visual form. They represent your absolute heart of magic; the symbols within are representative of the components of your paradigm. For example, one's Circle might have a pentagram, a five-pointed star. The pentagram might also include a symbol for each of the five suits of the Tarot, each within one of the star's points (the fifth suit naturally being the Trumps). In the center of that pentagram, we might place the back symbol on your Tarot deck. Use this as a default if you cannot think of your own unique Circle.

Some Circles are highly symmetrical, with precise and defined vectors for each symbol. Others are organic, drawn intuitively without an obvious boundary save for the outer rim. This is an entirely personal practice, and there aren't a lot of defined rules, outside personal preference or isolated tradition teaching. Feel free to use your own intuition and tradition methodology when designing your Circle.

The Circle is drawn as a circular boundary because of what it does. It delineates what exists in your world and is embraced by your Umbra, and what is cast out and left unmanifested. However, this is merely the Imago version of your Circle; there are Lingua versions of incantation one can use to cast a Circle of Art (see the Qabalistic Cross, the Hekas spell, or the Japanese kekkai spells for examples) as well as ways to Mirror your Circle through objects and such.

If you cannot draw the Magic Circle physically on the ground, you may draw it on cloth or paper, and use that as a placemat for your Weapons in the dedication ritual. Within the practice of the tradition you are learning in this book, the Sword goes in the North, the Wand in the South, with the Cup in the West and the Coin in the East. Please note, however, that your own practices may vary from this approach; use your own judgment when deciding placement. Once dedicated, the Cloth (or other implement of Fastness such as a reading board) will serve as your portable Magic Circle as well, so you can simply use that in the future.

SECONDARY EXERCISE: CREATING THE INCANTATIONS

To work with your Weapons, you'll need to develop three incantations:

- one to seal a Weapon to the Circle permanently;
- one to call upon and dedicate the Weapon to a wielder, which will only be used for the purposes of unlocking the powers of Cartomancy for a wielder aside from yourself;
- and finally one to call upon the Weapon as a vessel of the Light.

These incantations allow you to create your Weapons (and also your Regalia; these charms work for those tools as well) as vessels of power which can be passed down to your successor, while also attuning them so that they cannot be used easily by other sorcerers. Without the incantations, the tools are no better than any other object.

The practice of making one's incantations is a simple one, which draws upon the Magic Circle as a guide. Readers will note that these incantations are written in rhyme; this is not strictly necessary, but it is my preferred method. Primarily, this is because it is less about what the magician says, and more about what we mean. Remember - your incantations are Renaming the object. You will always finish with a key word that redefines the object. We will go more into incantation in a later chapter.

S. Rune Emerson

PREPARING THE RITE

You will need:

- *A chalice or bowl of water, wine, or other representation of the Cup, with a method of asperging or sprinkling said liquid*

- *A Wand or other representation of the Rod*

- *A bladed weapon or other representation of the Sword*

- *A bowl of coins, salt, or other representation of the currency of the Coin*

- *A cloth or working surface for your rite, which should act as a Fastness for your Rite - you can elevate it upon a table, or lay it upon the ground as you choose*

- *Your tarot deck*

- *Any other Regalia you seek to enchant: Fascinators, Talking Heads, Books, and Garb are all excellent choices.*

A note about this ritual:

You will notice that we use some of the tools before we consecrate them in this ritual. That first use is part of their dedication, and it precedes the actual consecration spells because these tools also act as foci for our Regard and our ability. Once the Rite is finished, the tools will be dedicated, and we shall have begun walking the path of Sorcery in earnest.

THE CHARMING OF THE SPACE

Begin by cleansing the space in whatever fashion is most appropriate to you. Burn incense, light candles, play music, and perform any personal cleansing rites you choose to perform. Stand in the center of your work place, and take up the Sword, speaking the following spell:

Word and blade, now draw the line
of truth, of Knowledge and of Care.
Bind Infernal and Divine,
to consecrate against despair.
Tween perfect Light and fertile Darkness,
these confines I give to Need.
Blessed against profane in every form -
in thought, in word, in deed.

Return the blade to the altar, and take up the Cup. Walk the circle clockwise, sprinkling water along the way. Speak these words:

Redden, ground, with blood of Art.
Charm the space and bless the Heart.
Courage rise, from Mirror'd sea -
We become the Mystery.

Return the chalice to the altar, and then pick up the Rod, and point first at the East, then South, then West, then North, repeating this incantation at each:

Gates of Image and design,
Open wide and thus align.
From these portals, pow'r instill -
All in service to our Will.

Point the Wand at the altar, and speak firmly:

By Arcana's open door
Might is wakened evermore.

Return the Wand to the altar, and take up the Coin. Walk the circle deosil a final time, and scatter a pinch/coin in the eight compass directions as you walk. Incant this verse:

Salt be salt, and gold be gold.
All in Silence, truth is told.
Cards of bounty, cards of Fate.
Here thy Body we create.

Finish your preparations with the following affirmation:

The Shadows are cast and thus remain,
Across time and space, in every plane.

S. Rune Emerson

†ñ€ LA𝖄IN؟ (ⴲF †ñ€ CARⴷ𝕊

Lay the Trumps of your deck in the following array of cards upon the working place of your Magic Circle, with the four Weapons standing at the four cardinal directions at the edge, and the other Regalia distributed evenly in accordance with your own internal design. Then, cast the first Incantation. Let all grow silent and quiet, and then speak the spell. When you are finished, you may remove your Weapons from the Circle, and clean up the cards. You may also burn the paper Circle if you made one, or you can store it somewhere safe if you wish. Chalk circles should be washed away for safety's sake.

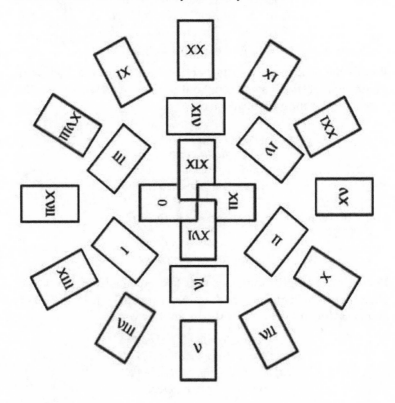

Please note: the numbers within this circle are based on the Trump order from the Rider Waite Smith deck, as that is the basis of our practice.

TO AWAKEN
THE CIRCLE OF CARDS

Circle born of Light and Dark -
The open Eye of my Regard.
Upon this ground I lay my Mark,
As both a focus and a ward.
By the Compass and the Crossroads,
And by Virtue's Sixfold Sign
I call upon the Magic Circle
and awaken what is mine.
So Mote It Be!

THE QUICKENING OF THE TOOLS

The following spells are used to awaken each of the four Weapons. The Regalia will have their own incantations later. For now, speak these incantations once each over each of the Weapons to awaken them to their purpose.

THE HERALDING INCANTATION:
(TO AWAKEN A WEAPON)

Body formed of Dark,
Power born of Light.
I conjure thee by Blood and Bone.
I conjure thee by Fire and Night.
Unto thee, oh (Weapon), now
let forces answer and be tame -
From this day let all awaken
and surrender to thy name.
(Name whispered 3 times)
So Mote It Be!

The Dedication: To Bind a Weapon to a Sorcerer

(Name of the Weapon), Hear me,
That Dark be moved by Light.
This Circle binds thee
with (sorcerer's name),
Forever joined in might.
So Mote It Be.

The Incantation of Wielding:
(Used Any Time the Weapon is Used)

Oh loyal Light which binds the Dark,
Your magic now be free.
By our Contract,
Thy might rise up
and Hearken unto me!
So Mote It Be!

Here you will notice three things: The Weapon was named - one must always name one's tools, for that is part of the encoding of the spell. Also, its name must only ever be used when binding it to the sorcerer, as its name can be used to affect it, and it is unwise to offer the closest reflections of one's treasures to untrustworthy ears.

The trigger words, "So Mote It Be" were used to unleash the spells being cast, which is a traditional sealing term for many magicians, although the magician may prefer to use their own words instead. A trigger phrase should always be used in a sorcerous incantation; that word is a Medium which affirms the forces of Light being unleashed upon the substance of the Dark.

The words of these incantations were affirmative in nature - they didn't request, nor did they leave room for argument. This is the proper way to form an incantation of sorcery, as the powers associated cannot move outside their norm without the force of a magician's will to move them.

Again, we will discuss incantation in further detail in a later chapter, but for now, let us press on.

HOW TO SUMMON AND BIND THE LIGHT

Once you have enchanted the Weapons, you will move onward to enchanting the Talking Head to make it into a proper portal through which the Lights of Sorcery may radiate forth. Place your hands over it, palms down, with your thumbs and forefingers touching so that you shape a triangle with your hands. Close your eyes and see rays of Light shining forth from three different places beyond your Circle, striking into the Head you have chosen and illuminating it, filling it with Light and opening a door to a place of magic. This realm is the world within your tarot deck, the secret realm beneath and around everything you see.

Speak the following incantation, with your eyes fixed in Regard upon the Head, seeing through it as a portal into that world:

> I spy by Light of Dawning Truth,
> A road through darkened sight.
> I spy by Light of Noontide Aid,
> A land of fertile might.
> I spy through Light of Dusk's Embrace
> A mist which hides it all.
> 'Tis there I stand by Midnight's grace,
> behind the Un-Light wall.

Take up the rest of your cards (not the Trumps) and shuffle them. Lay the first Cup you draw to its left, the first Coin to its right, the first Sword behind it, and the first Wand between you and it. Then, say the charm listed in the Talking Head section, repeated here for your convenience:

> Dawn for guidance,
> Noon for strength,
> Dusk for secrecy,
> And Night Take the Rest.

Light the Head if there is a light source within it, and pick up the cards around it. If there is not (or if you have already lit it), touch it or blow a kiss to it, and move on to the next consecration. It should be noted that the cards will not be needed to light the Head in the future, although one can lay the cards down again around a new Head to consecrate it subtly, and it will work as well as the original (if the original is still intact).

THE CHARM OF THE FASCINATOR

If the Talking Head is a portal to the world of your cards, then the Fascinator is a key to that portal. Enchanting it is fairly simple. Take up the cards (not the Trumps, but all the Minors) and shuffle them, and then draw a single card for the Fascinator, placed either above or beneath it. Speak the following charm:

> *All rooms have a door.*
> *All doors have a key.*
> *This Light I seal inside of thee.*
> *(Whisper its new name three times)*

It should be noted that the Fascinator's name changes based on what Light you trap inside it. In this case, it will be named after the card you've drawn for it, but its name will change when you've released the light of that card and bound something else within it.

Either way, place that card back in the deck. You're nearly finished.

THE MARKS OF BINDING

Consecrating your Book and the various components of your Fastness is actually a lot easier than you might think. It requires only two things: the ability to think in symbols, and the dedication of such symbols to a mystical code. Some people prefer to invent their own codes, whereas others prefer to use ciphers and magical alphabets or sigil systems already created, such as the runes of the Elder Futhark, or the letters of the Alphabet of the Magi.

In any case, you begin creating this system when you first

draw your Magic Circle; any emblems of Apparent Darkness you've placed into the Circle are part of your code. There are of course also symbols upon each of the cards of your deck. For example, if you use the five-petaled white rose of the Death card to stand for Death, then that is a symbol you might choose as part of your code.

To consecrate the Book, draw the Circle on the inside cover, on both sides. That will ensure that none not dedicated to the magic of your Circle can use the power of your Book. Once you have done this, name your Book by inscribing a title page.

Within the pages of your Book, the secret of your code will be found. You will need a symbol for each of the Trumps of your tarot deck, a symbol for each of the four suits of the Minor Arcana, and a symbol for each of the Pips and Courts. With these, you can lay your Mark upon objects and bind them to your Fastness. So long as you never explain these symbols, but keep them locked away in your Book, they will maintain the binding of your spells perfectly.

In any case, once you've sealed your Circle into your Book, the Rite is effectively over. You have consecrated your Weapons, charmed your Head and your Fascinator, and bound your Circle into your Regalia. You may now snuff any candles you may have lit, and take out any food offerings you wish to give to spirits you may have connected with. Let any incense you've lit burn its way out, and then break up any charcoal you may have used for it (if you use loose or cone incense and not sticks). Silence the music as well.

For a formal declaration of ending, you can close your Book after you've done all the rest, and say firmly:

Gates be closed to all but me -
the Rite is done.
So Mote It Be!

CHAPTER FOUR:
THE CARDS OF TRIUMPH

Among the cards of the Tarot, there are three different varieties of cards - the twenty-two cards of the Major Arcana known as the Trumps, the sixteen face cards of the Courts, and the four Aces and thirty-six other Pips, which together form the Lesser Arcana. In non-Tarot decks, one may find that the entire deck is comprised of what a tarologist would call Trumps, or Pips or Courts. This can be both incredibly useful and versatile for some work, and quite limiting in other ways. Remember that there is always a price to pay for each choice we make, and that includes the selection of a deck to work with. This is why we use a standard seventy-eight-card Rider Waite Smith Tarot deck as the base for this book's tradition.

As we begin our journey through the deck itself, please keep in mind the lore in this book about the cards is primarily intended to educate one in the arts of sorcery and cartomantic magic. There are a great many books written on the subject of the Tarot in its use for esoteric learning, divination, and even psychological profiling. Each of those books is valuable and valid for its purpose, and just as those books are loyal to systems such as the Qabala or the Golden Dawn, this book is written from the perspective of our own tradition of Cartomantic Sorcery.

The definitions found in this book are geared around the purpose of sorcery, and may not be entirely in synch with the definitions found by other authors. This is sometimes a reflection of differing lore, as there is a vast amount of information about the Tarot, and very little of its history is known. On occasion one will also find a difference of definition due to personal bias or differing paradigms - some do not believe in sorcery, strange as it sounds - others have their own revelations they wish to add, which prove counterproductive to the use of the Cards in our form of spellwork.

Above all, bear in mind that the Cards have their own mysteries, even deeper than those presented by this book or others. Had you not been intended to discover them and use them, you would never have found them. Magic has its own rules and laws, and in the realm of the subtle, there is always more to learn.

As our tradition of sorcery is built upon the foundation of tarot cartomancy, each of the following sections will educate you into the traditions of the Trionfi, which are also called Trumps or Triumphs. The 22 Trumps of the Tarot are greater secrets of magic. Each card's symbolism is layered with deep meaning in the style of medieval art. Each icon in the Rider Waite-based illustrations we are going to be using has a purpose and a meaning, and that meaning changes based on what you are looking for or asking about. Think of each card as a doorway through which one can pass, with Trumps acting as corridors of becoming and understanding. Any who cross the threshold of a Trump becomes that Trump.

In some traditions of Tarot reading, there is a practice known as the Fool's Journey, which is a method of divining and understanding one's own initiatory journey. We will conclude this chapter with an expanded method of using such a spread, adding both a method of dedication and a method of deepening the spread when using it as a divination.

Tħe four Paтħs of тħe Sorcerer's Ordeal

Of the Trumps, the first we shall discuss are the ones which are most important to our practice: those which educate the sorcerer on his practice and on the wyrd he shall follow. Sorcerers learn early on that there are four kinds of magic they shall be called upon to use in the service of themselves and others:

- the magic of Obscurity and Protection;
- the magic of Retribution and Balance;
- the magic of Understanding and Expiation;
- the magic of Gain and Assistance.

These four magicks are the Gold of our Sorcerer's Stone, which we seek to create in all we do. However, the ability to do so is not always easy. From the fickleness of a human heart to the constantly shifting nature of reality, it really can feel more like panning for Gold in murky rivers of being and becoming.

In the study of magic, all magicians undergo a time of trial and testing known as the Ordeal, a semi-involuntary crucible for their magic, the flame which forges their will into iron and tempers their being with wisdom and challenge. These trials are a natural manifestation of our own power, the forces we touch rebelling and challenging our ability to enforce our will. Each kind of magician's Ordeal is unique, and we shall concern ourselves with the shape of the Sorcerer's Ordeal in this book.

The trials of the Ordeal are not a punishment or penance, nor are they a sign that one should give up, or that what one is doing is wrong. Perhaps the strongest reason to discuss this particular concept early is so we can remind the magician that magic is not a practice for the weak or cowardly, and that a magician must accept that pain and sacrifice are simply part of the path. Recall the Eighth Law of Magic - Everything Has a Price. In order to gain, one must first give. In order to grow, one must feel the pain of growing. All choices and changes are costly, and the Ordeal is the method by which a magician naturally comes into their power. We will discuss this further, when we discuss initiation in a later section of this chapter.

Suffice to say that the Ordeal is more an ally than an enemy. Our Ordeal can do more than test our resolve; it can tell us about ourselves, and knowing ourselves is probably the first and most important lesson to learn.

A counsel for any magician experiencing the Ordeal can be found in the works of Eliphas Levi and his Four Powers of the Sphinx:

- Noscere - to Know, the act of mastering Faith by discerning what is factual from what is believed;
- Velle - to Will, the practice of mastering Hope through action in accordance with one's wish;
- Audere - to Dare, the method of mastering Fear through acceptance of risk and accountability;
- Tacere - to Be Silent, the way of mastering Doubt by embracing uncertainty with quiet resolve.

These methods afford any magician a sort of compass, which

guides us as we walk the labyrinthine pathways of our Ordeal. Holding to these tenets and facing each set of trials with them firmly in mind will transform seemingly daunting tasks into serendipitous events of significant benefit.

Keep these four tenets in mind as you read; each Pillar of the Pyramid corresponds to one of the cards below, and is the key to unraveling the secrets of that trial. The card and corresponding tenet may be your only aid in troubling circumstances.

THE FIRST TRIAL OF COMMITMENT: THE HANGED MAN

In the teachings of Peter Carroll, well known author on the subject of Chaos Magic, one finds this motto: "Nothing is true; everything is permitted."[4] This is a basic truth of all sorcery - if it was forbidden, it would be impossible. Sorcery is about changing the world according to our desires, and the Apparent freedom of this practice acts as smoke and cover for the other side of the coin.

Sorcery is a free magic, to be sure - yet all things have a price. For the sorcerer, one pays through the coin of devotion. If one would draw power from a Source, one must first give themselves to it. When a sorcerer first seeks to learn magic, they will find that the tools are hollow and the rituals frustrating, and they will go from place to place trying to find something, anything, which resonates for them. They will be endlessly frustrated by the incoherency and the lack of "truth" they find. Their lesson is that of the Hanged Man; it is less a matter of finding truth, and more a matter of paying for one's own beliefs and ideals. One must shed blood upon the Path of their own choosing before it will begin to guide them. A sorcerer must reach their pinnacle of frustration, and give up on all they believe, so that they may then know absence of the Light. When they learn this lesson, they will recognize the Light again where they find it, and they can then raise it up to illuminate their Path.

We call this trial the Trial of Seeking and Commitment, and it tests our Faith - our ability to hold fast in honor to that which is worthy, to give ourselves to something higher. Only then can we understand Truth, and Know the difference between it and Faith. By exercising our Faith, we learn that what we choose to believe in is not the Truth; it is merely the act which makes of us a worthy vessel for Knowledge. Faith is a beginning, not an ending.

THE SECOND TRIAL OF MIGHTINESS: THE TOWER

A sorcerer's will must be inviolate and unyielding. There is no room for weakness in magic, and even less in the magic of creation. The sorcerer will feel this deep in his soul. The power we call comes from the place inside of us which cries out at injustice and frustration, and howls an exultant "YES" when we gain purchase towards our desires. This spiritual zeal is what drives us; the faith we have invested allows no half measures, and it will not surrender us.

The world, however, has its own ideas of how things work. When we pick up our power finally, having committed ourselves fully to our Path, we then are faced with defeating that which stands against us. Like the lightning of the Tower, we are the force which destroys all which is based on falsehood. Our Light destroys that which would sabotage it. We must allow that to happen - the Light is both blessed and wrathful. Those who would stand with their Light will also find that same Light blinds others, or drives them mad.

This is a necessary and virtuous thing. None of us can exist in two contradictory worlds, and a man cannot serve two masters. A sorcerer must let their Will be iron forged by lightning, in order that they can become the Light of Hope for others seeking to find refuge from the storm of conflicting paradigms and worldviews. Only through strength and firmness, and an absolute and utter devotion to the truth, can one inspire and aid others or oneself. Therefore, it behooves us to maintain our commitment not only to ourselves and our desire, but to a higher vision, one we cannot see. We must simultaneously hold to the understanding that our will and wish are a good thing, and that a greater agency also acts in ways that we cannot see but can trust. We call this the Trial of Mightiness and Hardship, and it tests our Hope, for we are the Will which brings Hope to those around us, when they see nothing but destruction and despair. Through mastering our own suffering, we bring Light to others.

THE THIRD TRIAL OF NURTURING: THE FOOL

A sorcerer's might comes from their willingness to accept all possibilities as equal, to stack the odds and choose the outcome they desire. This is a difficult task, as Fear will often stand in the way of our ability to believe. When we desire an outcome, that desire often comes with the promise of despair should we not succeed. It can be terrifying to admit that kind of weakness.

It is not the nature of a sorcerer to accept failure or weakness. Willful stubbornness and pride are a common factor among magicians in general, and none so much as practitioners of sorcery. For us, there is no "our way or the highway," for there is no highway. The world must yield to our expectations; there is no other possibility.

In this, we see the wisdom of the Fool, who has committed themselves to an ideal and a set of morals, yet knows not the cost of such commitment. Sorcerers make many choices in our lives, and often we make foolish ones. Yet, because of our willingness to step past Fear and choose anyway, we often manage to succeed beyond any expectation.

The white dog at the Fool's feet is often called reason, but more appropriately it could be considered the power of Fear in its best aspect - a warning of danger, of cost, but a guardian and nothing more. This is known as the Trial of Nurturing and Sacrifice; a challenge to our Fear that causes it to become a force of aid to us instead of an obstacle. We choose to walk along the cliff, and Fear tells us that it is there. Through this, we accept freedom as our destiny, knowing that the hounding cry of Fear will warn us of danger, but that sometimes it will be worth the cost of the leap. Optimism coupled with healthy pragmatism are the way to success in sorcery, nearly all of the time.

THE FOURTH TRIAL OF VIRTUE: THE SUN

S. Rune Emerson

Magic changes those who practice it. This is a lesson known by every wise magician. When a sorcerer takes up their magic in earnest, committing themselves to it and learning to embrace their frailties, the power begins to change them. Usually, we take up sorcery as a selfish concern; we wish to triumph against adversity, to gain what we desire and achieve our dreams. However, the cost of practicing magic is becoming magical, and magic changes all it comes into contact with. By drinking the elixir of sorcery, we become an elixir ourselves.

The Sun is the closest (and to us, the brightest) of Stars. It burns with the Light of its Vision, and that Light will eventually be gone. Unlike other Stars, the Sun is not aloof and distant, inspiring from afar. Its power is near, and felt so potently by all on Earth that we even measure the passing of time by its movements. It can harm those who are unwise, but all can admit to its benign nature. Without the Sun, life on this planet would end in a very short time indeed.

The sorcerer is the same. Born of the Light of Vision, wielding the very might of creation, their power becomes their very nature and touches all who are nearby. That Light can harm, but it is by nature good, and its movements and absences will be felt. A sorcerer becomes more than just a wielder of a tool; they become the force of magic they use, and they cause change on levels they cannot even see. The Sun knows not that she is hot and bright, only that she is lonely and that she is herself. This is called the Trial of Virtue and the Mark, and it tests our ability to face Doubt and uncertainty with Silence. As the Sun shines by Virtue of her nature, so do we. What we are is undeniably good, and this is something we must accept even in the face of Doubt. It can be hard to commit oneself to being a force of good, and harder still to accept it. We must learn to follow our Light, to celebrate Virtue in ourselves and everything, and let the Light change as it is wont to do.

In the Light,
there is Surrender.
In Surrender,
there is Strength.
In Strength,
there is Freedom.
In Freedom,
there is Joy.
In Joy,
there
is
Light.

S. Rune Emerson

ThE SIX LIGHTS OF INITIATION

In magic of all kinds, one uses subtle and Unseen forces to manipulate Apparent reality. It is a game of bait and switch in many cases, but not because there is no substance to magic; quite the opposite, in fact. A magician hides their Art behind smoke and mirrors because the power we wield can be unraveled and turned against us, the secrets stolen and misused. Thus, we learn one major rule - if something is unimportant, turn it into a spectacle. If something is crucial, distract attention away from it. Remember this, for it will aid you.

In the practice of magical misdirection, one of the common things to hide is the source of one's power. Now, as we discussed previously in this book, magicians conduct power through a Medium, a conduit of a source of magic. Terms like "spirit" or "energy" are used to explain the force we conduct in many circles. Within the confines of our Cartomantic Sorcery tradition, we prefer to use the term "Light," due to the ancient traditions of the old astrologers and magi, and also due to the relevance it has upon this tradition. This also has associations with the concept of the Divine, which is very likely the first form of Light any human sorcerer ever had cause to understand. In truth, what we call Divine Light is the heart of all magical power, the very first Source. We saw our gods shaped of it, and we saw it in all things we considered special or sacred. This force is the true Source of all cartomantic sorcery (and probably all magic in all honesty), and as such, we can infer that all magic is at its core good, and that the only "evil" magic is a magic which denies this Divinity (whether seen in a secular fashion or a religious one) as its basis.

In our paradigm of Cartomantic Sorcery, we refer to magical change as the Light shaping the Dark. Light is bound and shaped according to the design of the cartomancer, and the Dark is therefore reified, renamed, that it may now take the form of the magician's desire. However, much of the bulk of magic is performed not only by magicians, but by all of nature. The process which births the mortal Darkness into a form capable of channeling the Light of magic, for example, is the same for all things in Creation. That which makes an herb capable of being used for bewitchment or poison is the same process which makes a sorcerer able to cast her spells.

The processes by which one is brought into being a Medium for power, called Initiation by the old practitioners of the Art, are six in number. Each of the six processes of Initiation are symbolized by one of the Trumps, and are explained in further detail in this section. Remember, these methods are not merely for making an object magical; they can be used to craft a moment into magic, and also to shape oneself into a greater Medium for the Light of Creation.

As sorcery is a magic of redefinition and re-identification, the process by which the Divine Light is unleashed is one of renaming in and of itself, and therefore the six ways of Initiation are also the names of six Sources of power, which we shall identify here:

1. Infernal, that which defies the natural order
2. Faery, that which creates contradiction and paradoxical truth out of order
3. Necromantic, that which has gone beyond reach of natural order
4. Elemental, that which enforces the natural order
5. Primal, that which utilizes the atavistic chaos within order
6. Astral, that which exists eternally beyond the natural order

With these six generic concepts as a template for the myriad Sources one can encounter through their Initiatory Mediums, we can begin to harness the Light of Creation and work with it in our sorcery. We will discuss the six archetypal concepts of Initiation in the following pages.

THE MAGICIAN:
THE LIGHT OF THE RIDDLE

The first process of Initiation into power we shall discuss is, perhaps, the most important to any practitioner of magic: the practice of the Riddle. All magicians of any kind must learn to see through the illusions of reality and to interact with the subtle and Unseen. However, it is not enough to see through that facade. One must then decide to take up the raw force they perceive on the other side of the veil, and begin to shape it into tools.

Each magician, be they sorcerer, witch, or wizard, must set forth to harness the powers of magic to their own ends and ideals. This choice is symbolized by the Magician, the teacher of the power Infernal. A magician's will is adversarial, challenging, and clever; it flies in the face of the constants of the world, and tricks it into changing itself through cleverness, guile, and outright confrontation. The Magician's card teaches us to be willful, to be clever and attentive, and to make things turn out the way we wish because we will it so. It teaches us skill and versatility.

As a process of Initiation, it brings forth the Light by pitting one against one's own opposite, forcing us to see truth or submit. The Ordeal is often this force in action - it tempers us, teaches us, and brings us forward that we may realize key understandings about the world around us. It teaches us that magic happens in many cases because we will it to, because we decide it to. A stuffed doll becomes a guardian, a candle becomes a blessing, a piece of string becomes a twisting of the threads of Fate itself, all because we have learned a secret and have chosen to use it.

The Magician teaches the fourfold axiom known as the Riddle of the Sphinx: be wise, be willful, be brave, and be silent.

THE HIGH PRIESTESS:
THE LIGHT OF THE QUEST

Some magic is born into this world because of how it is perceived. An herb may have power based on its nature, but it may also become powerful by virtue of how it is sought and collected. If enough mystique surrounds the acquisition of something, that mystique has the power to produce magic by virtue of the wonder and trepidation it inspires. This is why many magicians keep secrets; they can draw strength not only from the Light within a piece of secret knowledge, but also from the very act of keeping a secret and making it difficult to find.

This is represented in the Trumps by the High Priestess, she who keeps the gateway through the veil of Mystery. A Mystery is something one cannot understand unless one experiences it; it cannot be expressed or explained to any who have not also experienced the Mystery. A sorcerer can claim this magic by making her actions wondrous and strange, eccentric even to the point of being confusing. She can wield the force of curiosity and confusion as a force which baffles and contradicts. The mists of the realm of Faery, the strangeness of the inexplicable, are a power to wield, and a force which Initiates all it touches.

The Priestess counsels without explaining, and those who seek her power do the same. One does not need to make sense. One must simply follow the path and experience what is there. Logic, after all, isn't always truth, and not all truths can be unraveled by thinking. We find echoes of this in the words of Herman Slater and Ed Buczynski, who founded Earth Religion News: "Guard the Mysteries. Reveal them Constantly."[5] The paradox of this statement is an affirmation of the High Priestess' wisdom: never explain, but reveal. Deepen the magic. Do not cheapen it.

THE EMPRESS:
THE LIGHT OF TRANSITION

Sometimes a Medium becomes powerful not through its use or its nature, but rather through what happens to it. Fate, destiny, karma - these are terms which explain something we cannot really explain. All of the mortal world is affected by, and has an effect upon, everything in the mortal world. And, by Virtue of being mortal, all things die.

Death, of course, is no serious difficulty to the immortal forces we wield; it is merely a transformation, an enchantment as we will discuss later. However, it does convey one into a new existence, and that can bring forth the capacity to conduct Light in one way or another. After all, death is merely a change, a Light shaping the Dark. That same Light may transform the mortal Darkness into a form capable of conducting the Light which shaped it. Many shamanic traditions speak of the Rite of Death and Rebirth as a form of Initiation. So too, many people with psychic powers have spoken of having a near-death experience which sharpened their gifts and senses.

In any case, this process of Initiation is attended by the Empress, the subtle hand of guidance and nurturing, the gardener and caretaker of all mortal lives. She is the keeper of the magic of death, and it is she who gently guides us all through our lives and choices unto our appointed end. No spectre of evil or villainy, she is compassionate. She shows mercy and aid to those who must change, for such is the Law - all things change, and there must be harmony and balance in it. And indeed, the immortal cannot die; only the transitory can experience transition. The Light shall always move the Dark, and the Light shall always answer the call of a Medium which can channel its might, even if it be in ways Necromantic. Trust in fate and have faith; let the world mark you.

THE EMPEROR:
THE LIGHT OF SOVEREIGNTY

Sorcery is the practice of redefining the universe in accordance with one's own principles, beliefs, and vision. By interacting with the subtle powers of creation, we deify ourselves and place the crown of sovereignty upon our own head. However, by doing so, we can sometimes fall prey to the delusion that we have made an original decision, that this was not inherently the plan to begin with. We forget that we too are creatures of nature; even our ability and aptitude for sorcery is an innate quality of our nature, and therefore is part of the grand design.

Magic is not a cheat. Magic is the law of nature in action. In the study of the Art, magicians have discovered various mystical properties inherent in curios such as plants, stones, metals, and in certain words, actions, or even in the passing of time. These Elemental properties can be used in magic as Mediums of power, and they also can be learned from as lessons of the necessity of the world. Magic works because it must, and it is a much needed law of the universe. Therefore, magic is ever-present and intrinsic, and holds sovereign authority over everything in creation. All things are magical because they must be magical.

The card which represents this concept is the Emperor, both for the idea of imposed order which a sorcerer brings to the table, and also for the wisdom it grants us. Even a bad king is better than no king. Even a stupid or poorly-trained sorcerer is better than having no hope for change at all. Truly, the study of sorcery isn't even about the changing of things. It's about the understanding of how things become what their destiny intends for them. Magic is not about getting what we want. It's about being what we are, what we were born to be. It's up to us to put the right work in, if we want to actually be able to achieve any of our goals.

THE LOVERS:
THE LIGHT OF RESONANCE

Magic resonates, and like attracts like. That which we seek, we do so out of profound desire and emotion. This is a path to power; intimacy with a source of Light is what makes something a Medium. However, it is not enough to grow close in proximity. One must also grow close in affinity. One must draw close to the Light because one seeks and needs it. One must desire what it can provide or what one can experience from it. This is the grand illusion created by this process - the idea that one can find what one seeks, in the breath and being of another.

The Lovers card is one of choice, like the Magician. However, it has a very singular difference. Where the Magician speaks of willful choice and sacrifice, the Lovers represents a choice that cannot be made in the field where it is shown. When one chooses a lover, one does not truly choose the other person. One chooses oneself, and what one experiences and feels with that lover. One chooses one's own Light.

This way of Initiation is one born of love and desire and affection; even objects without conscience can reach the kind of Resonance spoken of in the Lovers. Two stones may have great affinity for each other, and after long years in each other's company, they can be used to find each other, and may even be able to channel each other's Light. On this road, it is not a matter of time or transition, but rather the affirmation of natural resonance and intimacy. The souls within the stones recognize and complement each other naturally without changing. This is as clean and clear an example of this principle as we can muster. Learning from it, we learn to let our emotions be clear and Primal, so that we may resonate with a force of Light in each and every moment.

TEMPERANCE:
THE LIGHT OF PARADIGM

All things experience change, and all things are what they are. These are truths, and ways of magic. However, Creation is a mixture of individual components adding to a great whole, an Astral soup within a cauldron which blends Order and Chaos into scintillating Dream. It is the work of the magician to blend the strange and the commonplace, so that what is bizarre becomes status quo. Unfortunately, this comes with a great burden - that of Paradox, of conflict and contradiction. When a sorcerer redefines the world, they do so backwards and forwards through time. What they reify becomes reality as it has ever been. However, within the sorcerer lies the memory of the previous reality, held just as rigidly as the new world. This becomes a problem, as the magician then becomes a vessel which holds two contradicting truths, a Medium which resonates with opposing Lights.

Thus the work of Alchemy, the magic of moderation. From the Temperance card, we learn to balance these contrasting visions by mixing and blending them together, so that they become one great Paradigm of manifold facets and images. A sorcerer must find ways to create or even become the bridge which harmonizes all disparate forces. This is the largest difficulty of our work - how to know truth when it flies in the face of our vision, and how to make that Light work for us. This is not merely the experience of a magician, either; it manifests in tantalizing moments all throughout nature. Those moments of pure Gold, of immortal divine bliss... those are what we as magicians seek our entire lives. Immortality. Sublime reality. Perfection. The Divine is everywhere and in everything - in every work of art, in every exquisite manifestation of nature. It exists in the study in contrasts and evolution through ordeal and triumph, and in the observation of a life cycle. Those who practice Alchemy spend their lives seeking to bring forth that perfection from out of base earth. Called the Philosopher's Stone or, more relevantly, the Sorcerer's Stone, it is the bringer of perfection, of Lead into Gold, of dross into divinity, of Paradox into Paradigm. It is the perfect elixir - and each spell and object of enchantment we fashion, we do so with this vision in mind.

The Twelve Beacons of The Arte Magical

Sorcerous spellcasting is actually really simple. We've discussed the four Rules of Sorcerous Arte already, and they're really quite easy to follow. Find a Source of Light conducted through a Medium, act in a way that Reflects and portrays the change, and Rename the subject in accordance with your Will, Wish, and Surrender.

However, while the mechanism is simple, one still needs education into what one is capable of doing. Magic can create effects that may seem impossible to the uneducated, but it does have its limits, both on what it cannot do and what it can and is likely to accomplish. The practice of learning these intricacies are the bulk of the study of what is called the Arte Magical, the intuitive and artistic aspect of magical practice. Each of the different categories of Arte Magical are like colors upon a palette, and a magician mixes and blends them to create the effects they desire.

In truth, the Artes of magic are manifold; we use the subtle forces of nature to create change in the world. Much of what we do is raw and free, and cannot be pinned down. However, there are a few limits to what we are capable of, and it is important to understand one's limitations, else one cannot surpass them.

Some simple limits to a magician's powers (as mentioned in previous chapters) may be codified thus:

Magicians cannot touch the will directly; they can only affect that which surrounds the will. We can bend the flesh, change the spirit, and influence the heart and mind. But those are merely circumstances, and they are always subject to change. What we cannot do is touch the soul, the seat of divine power within anything. We may make one thirsty, but we cannot make them drink.

A magician is not a god. They are as mortal as any other in this world. They must sleep, eat, and drink, and they are confined by the limits of their mortal existence and understanding. Therefore, their spells will always have holes in them, and there will always be something they did not think of.

This is normal and natural, although we may spend a lifetime trying to surpass it.

The magic of a magician is magic of the mortal world, and must function according to natural law. No spell will defy physics or the greater laws of Creation. That spell which seems to defy the ways of the world is merely upholding another way within the order of Reality. One cannot counteract a force without an equal force opposing it, after all.

Keeping these limitations firmly in mind will help one keep from making "rookie" mistakes. Every magician in the world dreams of telekinesis and fireballs and teleportation, and these are lovely fantasies. There's nothing which says they're strictly impossible, either. Unfortunately, the province of creating such effects lies firmly in the realm of practical science, rather than the mystical arts of sorcery. Science operates upon the physical, magic upon the metaphysical. What empirical effects we create are entirely formed by the influence of the Unseen upon the Apparent, which is somewhat more useful than one might think.

After all, being able to levitate objects with the power of one's mind is entertaining, but if the only trick one has is to make an object move, that's rather limited. However, if one's magic can make objects move, people change their thoughts, and weather patterns create strange effects all to further a single goal (such as one's own good fortune or health), through the wise and clever use of a single spell, how much greater is the scope of one's magical potential?

Aside from a few basic rules about what magicians cannot do, there are a few guidelines within the Arte Magical as to what we can accomplish. Chiefly, there are twelve standard practices within the Arte Magical - twelve effects any magician can bring into being. These are known to our Cartomantic Sorcery tradition as the Twelve Artes, as we have already begun to mention. The Twelve Artes are the standard for basic thaumaturgy, that is to say, an empirical effect produced through the channeling of Light through a Medium to some purpose.

While the Twelve Artes are merely a model for one's mental organization, they serve well as a focus of study. A savvy student will use a model to help them practice, setting up experiments and workings within each Arte, so that they can become proficient in each.

Indeed, becoming proficient in the Twelve Artes is the work of any apprentice or student, for until one can produce results in all of the basic ways of sorcery, one cannot begin the true work of a sorcerer - the discovery of what we call the Thirteenth Arte, the unique interpretation of magic that is one's own addition to the great body of the Arte Magical. This Thirteenth Arte is the crowning glory of each magician: a unique magic that is born of their own paradigm, which transcends all the seeming limits of the Arte and makes one a true Master.

In any case, the Twelve Artes are listed here in the order of their alignment with the Four Manifestations:

The Three Artes of Fate:

- ◦ Luckbending, also known as hexing, which is the Arte of bending Fate and changing luck
- ◦ Divination, the practice of reading the twists and patterns of Fate, thereby learning hidden things
- ◦ Conjuration, the Arte of summoning or banishing the things of the mortal world by Fate and Will

The Three Artes of Power:

- ◦ Evocation, the unleashing of a spirit from its sleeping place, sending power out to do one's bidding
- ◦ Invocation, the drawing in of power and spirit from the immortal realms, to wear its mantle
- ◦ Abjuration, the ways of binding and warding the spiritual forces which one encounters

The Three Artes of Mystery:

- ◦ Glamoury, the practice of illusion and befuddlement, influencing the senses and memories
- ◦ Compulsion, the Arte of bidding and persuasion, by which other spirits may be swayed
- ◦ Enchantment, the Arte of blessing, cursing, and magical transformation

THE THREE ARTES OF NECESSITY:

- ◦ True Sight, the vision which plucks truth from all it perceives, Unseen or Apparent
- ◦ Healing, the use of natural processes of Necessity and flesh to bring aid, alteration, or affliction
- ◦ Weather Working, the manipulation of nature's balance to a specific end, such as summoning rain

These magicks are each heralded by one of the remaining twelve Greater Arcana, and their corresponding Trump is the gateway to understanding the secrets of that magical action. We shall go over each one in detail in the following pages.

LUCKBENDING: TURNING THE WHEEL OF FORTUNE

The first Arte we will discuss is Luckbending, also known as hexing or "the evil eye," a practice used by magical practitioners to bend the factors of a particular outcome in one way or another. Bending which sides a pair of dice might show, bending the immune system of a foe so that they become sick, bending the road of a child so that they avoid danger - all of these are potential uses of Luckbending. However, in order to come to an understanding of how to adequately use such a power, one must first learn what is really happening, on a visceral level.

In the Wheel of Fortune in the classic Rider Waite Smith deck, the card is depicted with seven creatures - a set of four at the corners of the card, including an eagle, a lion, a bull, and a man; in the center of the card adorning the Wheel itself, one finds a jackal-headed man, a serpent, and a sphinx. Any student of Hermetic lore can discover that the four beasts on the outer corners are meant to represent the four aspects of the sphinx in the center; and we can further assess that the sphinx is symbolic of the Riddle aforementioned in this book, with each of those beasts representing one of the Pillars of the Riddle: to Know, to Dare, to Will, and to Be Silent.

However, the deep message of this card is much more interesting, when we apply it to the purpose of sorcery, chiefly when we seek to learn to bend luck and fate to our desire. All four of the beasts on the outer corners are totemic and primal, including the man; each represents a mystery which is neither good nor evil. In the center, we have the jackal-headed god Anubis, who guards the gates of death. We have the serpent Typhon (or Apophis), who is said to be a god of darkness and wickedness and disorder. And, we have the Sphinx, who herself is the guardian of the great Riddle which separates man from mage.

This is meant to convey a powerful lesson - the twists of Fate are not meant to be known, nor does a wise person take them personally. We may one day soar like an eagle, and the next day bear the burden of the ox. We may be wise as a man, or fierce as a lion. And none of these are bad or wrong. So too, those who would seek to harness the powers of the sorcerer's gaze must pass through tests. They must understand the nature of the power. The three Guardians of the Wheel are the trials one must face, the mysteries one must be initiated into. For it is in their nature and their being where we may find the secret of the use of such power, and the motives which serve as Medium. Only one who understands Fate can wield it.

The real secret to Luckbending within the Wheel of Fortune lies in understanding those Guardians. Apophis is the serpent of evil in Egyptian lore, and all forms of worship involving Apophis are apotropaic, designed to destroy evil influences by destroying or acting against Apophis in some way. In terms of Luckbending, that tells us that the power to hex and cast malevolent forces are one of the ways this Arte manifests. We also see Anubis, the Guardian of the gates of the Egyptian Underworld, one who ushered souls to be weighed. In this, we see the power of the Eye as Judge, weighing and measuring and acting in accord with the heart.

Finally, we see the Sphinx, and in the Sphinx we see the four beasts situated in the corners of the card: eagle, bull, lion, and man. This is a riddle, to be sure, and as such is a symbol of the Magician's path of initiation. However, it also hints at a deeper purpose. Each of those beasts comprises the Sphinx who is the symbol of wisdom and secretkeeping, and also is an emblem for magic-users everywhere. Perchance, each beast represents an act of willful Luckbending - the eagle with the power to grant something swiftness, or the bull to stand against adversity.

In any case, the card teaches its magic through discovery, and when one is finished learning its lesson, one will possess a greater understanding of how the weight of one's Regard is used.

TO LAY THE SPHINX'S EYE

The Wheel turns, and all are turned,
and Fate is once again rewoven,
that new lessons can be learned,
and Tricks be played, and hearts be
proven.

If ye'd cast with Fortune's lore,
let Hand choose one of gestures four -
Claw to rend and horn to score,
Palm to catch and wing to soar

Then let thine Eye in firm regard
descend upon thy subject hard,
be they good friend or foe untoward,
As ye behold, so does the card.

Thy Light through Wheel's beacon pierce
and with thy heart and reason fierce,
pronounce their Fate with Eye held fast
And by thy judgment, spell be cast.

DIVINATION:
THE DEVIL'S COUNSEL

Quite probably the most obvious and commonly-accepted use of Cartomancy in this modern age is the practice of divination - the Arte of delving into the hidden wisdom, drawing forth secrets and truth from the realms of obscurity. Nearly everyone in the world of today has heard of fortune-telling; horoscopy, tarot reading, and numerology are present everywhere. They are incorporated into our stories, our religions, even our everyday decisions. This is by no means a new practice; divination as a way of life has been recorded as being practiced for centuries, with signs suggesting that regular practice of divination may have been standard up to 14,000 years ago. Divination has long been a part of the human experience.

However, divining and auguring have also long been associated with evil and heresy. The greatest of the Hebrew kings, Solomon the Wise, was said to have declared all forms of divination forbidden in his kingdom (apart from the prophesying done by his own priests under his watchful eye). The Judeo-Christian holy books, as well as the Islamic Quran, expressly forbid the use of divination, or the speaking of prophecy, and the seeking of oracles. Indeed, one of the most common methods of divination was bastardized to be synonymous with evil magic; the practice of necromancy, which is the consultation of the dead for knowledge and wisdom, became an epithet of malevolence on par with the malignancy often associated with the terms "sorcery" or "witchcraft," and with just as sparse justification.

Nevertheless, one must be wise when one seeks wisdom from the omens of Fate. Remember, one must first understand Fate if one would wield it. The card associated with divination is the Devil - the one figure from the Bible who never lied, yet is called the Father of Lies. This is because the Devil uses truth to corrupt; when truth is sought, he speaks it in such a way that the natural flaws in a person's understanding deceive the heart and mind. The same scrupulous self-introspection and humble resolve needed to summon a demon are what one must have to practice divination.

The figures on the card are reminiscent of this. The souls of two human beings, one male, one female, are chained to the throne of the Devil - one consumed by the fire of zealous obsession, the other tempted by the fruits of excess. The Devil himself brandishes an ancient Judaic sign of benediction, which many believe represents his heresy and transgression against the holy signs of the divine. However, the secret to be learned here is actually manifest in the very appearance of the card. The Devil is not your friend, but neither is he your enemy. He shows the sign of benediction (the same one stolen by Leonard Nimoy for Vulcan use in Star Trek) to remind you that he too is sacred. In fact, all he offers is the truth; it is our flaws which seduce and deceive us, not his words.

Bear this in mind when practicing divination; the Devil is a card of truth. Unfortunately we are not always truthful with ourselves and others. This is why it is imperative for sorcerers to be constantly vigilant over their own balance, so as not to fall prey to excess and zeal.

If one observes closely, the Devil bears an inverted resemblance to the Lovers card - two figures, with an angel standing between them, one blessed with fire, the other with fruit. This is because he too represents a choice - the choice to accept truth and allow oneself to be cleansed, or to resist the truth and thereby be conquered.

This is the true power of divination - truth is a power which cannot be thwarted. It is inevitable and implacable, and it does not forgive. However, if we let it humble us all while remaining focused on our dreams, we will learn that the chains are not tight, and we can walk away freely, bearing the freedom of having truly learned from truth. That is what divination is for - learning and being liberated.

TO COMPEL TRUTH FROM FATE

1.
*Words mislead,
and foes deceive.
Deception goads
the heart to grieve.*

4.
*Thrice around,
a circle walk,
move widdershins,
their lies to mock.*

3.
*Then to the Devil,
give all lies,
and take up wisdom
as thy prize.*

2
*If ye would know,
what truth is hidden,
and what knowledge
is forbidden,*

5.
*If ye have offered from the heart,
then truth shall out in every part.
and ye will see by omens dire,
when lies around thee do conspire.*

CONJURATION:
THE FATE OF THE WORLD

Magic is ever present. The universe we live in is a tapestry of shadows woven by Light out of primal Darkness. When a sorcerer casts a spell to bring something into existence, he parts the shadows which veil our eyes, and lets the Light reveal what was in the Dark, making the Unseen Apparent.

To conjure is to bring something into existence, to draw it out of the Dark. When a sorcerer seeks an omen, he often will conjure an oracle from the world. When he desires an outcome, often he can raise it from the formlessness of the Unseen and bring it into being. The arts of Conjuration are about bringing about the world one desires, whether that means banishing away that which is unwanted, or summoning what is missing into one's sphere.

The World card in the Rider Waite Smith deck depicts a woman, naked, a Wand such as the one held by the Magician in either hand. Around her is a wreath of green leaves, bound by red ribbon. At the four corners of the World, we find the four beasts found upon the Wheel card - the Eagle, the Lion, the Bull, and the Man. Indeed, the similarities between the Wheel and the World are striking, making it entirely unsurprising that they are related by virtue of their mutual association with Fate.

Unlike the Wheel's impersonal association with Fate in the form of luck and destiny, the World implies control and the ability to dance with the twists and turns of fortune. That is because this card focuses on the concept of Gain - a world exactly as one desires.

The wreath implies not only success and victory, though it is traditional as a sign of triumph in Renaissance and medieval times. It also acts as a border, a Magic Circle as we have described previously. Its resemblance to a portal of passage, and also as a hedge of boundary, is obvious to the eye which seeks the Hidden. Indeed, in other versions of the card, that wreath is an ouroboros serpent, a clear sign of Initiation and Mystery.

Her nudity describes her freedom, and the scarf is a sign of joy. Indeed, to conjure, one must cast from joy. The Wands show her control, her ability to shape her environment to match the Image of her desire.

The beasts, however, remind us to acknowledge that the realm we live in, though we master its shape, still has its own existence outside of our ideals. This will be no simple undertaking, but rather a constant dance of Creation. For that is the key of all true Sorcery; we create our reality, every day, and the dance is never-ending.

The four beasts who stand for the Four Corners of the Earth and Sky, therefore representing everything in heaven and earth, are the spirits which educate us and initiate us into the magicks of conjuration - summoning and banishing, joining and separating. And, due to this card's connection to the power of Fate, we can also know that its magic is geared toward managing our Circle through guiding and commanding Fate.

The spirits, immortal and untouched by Fate, stand outside the Circle. Keep that in mind; nothing unbound by Fate can be conjured, only those things which dwell within the Mortal sphere. Dance with the World, and wield her two Wands of Desire and Discernment, and shape the entirety of your own realm to meet your expectations.

To Transport An Object

A Name a circle round
thy subject
tread.

Defined
by   Light
and   thy
true   wish
said.

Thy
spell shall
make their Fate become winged.

And to thy destination they'll be sped.

EVOCATION:
THE TAMING OF THE BEAST

Evocation: the power to call forth the immortal powers and unleash them. The might of the gods and demons, the secrets of the muses and the angels, all at our fingertips. One might say that this is the greatest joy of practicing sorcery: the ability to converse and trade with the spirits which daily make and remake the world. Through evocation, we can call upon and bring forth the primal spirits and "energies" of life, shaping them into new forms and bending the shadows of the world to our will.

However, the practice of evoking is deceptively simple. It requires very little to call forth power, because all the work is done beforehand in the heart of the magician. Sorcerous evocations are powerful things, and also versatile. One could as easily call forth a spirit of healing as a spirit of rage and vengeance; all spirits have their place in Creation. Likewise, one could draw forth elemental Fire for benign purposes or fell, to be shaped by one's own heart.

Yet this is not as easy as it sounds, for no amount of training of the mind will serve a mage seeking to master evocation. This is because the true secret dwells not within the signs and symbols, nor in the desire of the mage, but in the purity of his or her emotions, in the clarity of their heart.

Observe the card of Strength, for example. Here, a woman stands with a lion's head held gently in her hands. The lion seems to show affection to her. Above her head hovers the lemniscate, the endless knot of infinity. Her gown is white for purity, and she is dressed with signs of bounty, showing that she is good at what she does.

The relationship between the woman and the lion is one of submission, she to the power which moves through her, and he to her will. She closes his mouth firmly, as they Regard each other. The force of the infinite Light flows through her in purity, making of her a Medium of magic.

This is the key to Evocation - one must be a channel for Power if one seeks to move it. Remember, the Light cannot turn upon itself. Spirits and occult Powers are born of particular emanations of Light, and one must understand and wield the Light firmly in order to direct such forces. It is the strength of one's will which then holds the proverbial maw of the lion closed; the force one unleashes is directed no longer by its previous fetters but by those of the magician's will and that alone.

Within the three cards of the Artes of Power, one can find similar themes of this as a constant. Being a conduit of power, a Medium oneself, is a major part of working with Power in general. So too, the managing of Power is an act of resolve and will, and one must be firm in one's understanding of one's heart and one's desire and authority in order to command a force of Power to one's bidding directly.

In truth, this is often why the Triangle of Art is often portrayed in Magic Circles - as a reminder to the magician and the spirit she summons just exactly what that spirit is answering to.

TO CALL A FAMILIAR

Named and drawn,
a pact of friends,
never broken.

Around a triangle place each,
and from card body, ye beseech.
By threefold gift, call for thy friend.
When named and drawn,
they shall attend.

Card for face,
icon chosen,
never spoken.

Sigil drawn
of thy design
as a token.

THE HIEROPHANT: INVOKING THE MOST HIGH

The card which teaches Invocation is the Hierophant, which is a word for one who interprets the deeper mysteries and conveys them to the populace. Depicted in the card, we have a central priestly figure who wears many ecclesiastical garments, and is gesturing ritualistically over two tonsured monks at his feet. Crossed between them are two keys, and each monk wears a different robe - one with roses, another with lilies.

The meaning behind these symbols is actually easy to understand. The garb worn by the priest (and the throne) describe the practices of Invocation known as "aspecting" and "mantling," the assumption of the intelligence, authority, and gifts of an occult Power. Clearly depicting someone similar to the Pope, the Hierophant speaks *ex cathedra* as the Pope does. The monks wear the garb of life and death, showing the Hierophant's command of both, as emissary and speaker for a Power of the universe. Likewise, the crossed keys are the keys to the gates of Heaven (the realm of the Light the Hierophant is channeling). They bespeak the ability to bind and loose the Power wielded by the Hierophant. The tools held by the Hierophant are also symbols of authority, the crozier and the triregnum crown, all of which represent the right to command.

You may have noticed that I avoid speaking the gender of the Hierophant. That is because some old stories state that the Rider Waite Smith deck's Hierophant is actually the High Priestess in disguise, perhaps intending to remind us of the stories of Pope Joan, the woman whose disguise as a priest was so good that she was elected Pope and nobody knew she was a woman until she gave birth. Whether there is any accuracy to that story or not is irrelevant. The Hierophant is a figure whose gender is irrelevant, for anyone can call the Light in whatever form they choose, and all of us can make of ourselves a vessel for the Most High.

Wrapped in the clothes of the Power she (or he) wields, the Hierophant gives us a hint or two about how to invoke properly. Seated on the throne, she shows us to sit firmly in the authority of the Power we invoke. We are encouraged to wear the signs of that Power's nature and dominion, and to remain in firm connection with its nature.

The gesture of the Hierophant is the sign of benediction and blessing, a hallowing gesture. From this, we can understand one of the jobs of a vessel of Light is to convey that Light into the darkened places where it is needed most. The crozier carried in the Hierophant's left hand is the sign of one's responsibility to what one wields. We do not possess the Power; it moves through us, and channeling it means we bear the responsibility of what is done with it, and what is needed from it.

Invocation is a manifold practice, ranging from the leaching effects of psychic vampirism to the full-on possession of the vodouisants and their lwa. The symbols and figures on the Hierophant's card show us each in precise detail, leading to the ultimate ideal practice of assumption, which conveys wisdom and authority to those who invoke, in exchange for service to the greater purpose of the Power invoked.

ＴＯ ＩＮＶＯＫＥ ＴＨＥ ＬＩＧＨＴ

```
      C                          T                        T
      R                          H                        I
C R O S S                T H R E E                T I M E S
      S                          E                        E
      S                          E                        S
```

And then proclaim
thyself with mantle
thrice renamed.

Always in honor
to the Source
whose Will in Union
ye enforce.

Once for Guidance,
Once for Might,
Once for Aid,
Become the Light.

THE CHARIOT:
THE REINS OF ABJURATION

The Chariot is a card of interesting complexity; it describes duality in tandem, the unity of dichotomy to achieve a greater goal. Its symbolism, from the two sphinxes (traditionally one black and one white), to the banner of the Lingam and Yoni, all depict duality in conjunction under a higher authority.

So too can be seen the practice of Abjuration, the binding and warding of Power into patterns we desire. Whether we inhibit action (known as binding) or prohibit entry (known as warding), we recognize that Power (and the Arte of Abjuration in general) is dualistic as sorcery itself is dualistic, describing an in and an out, a yes and a no.

So also, one sees paradox in action - the card's name is not the Charioteer, but the Chariot. The human agency is less important in this card, merely a vessel of the Power. This time, however, the Power is manifest as a conveyance, something used to get the human figure where he needs to go. Power will be harnessed and bound to a purpose, to protect the charioteer as he journeys, and to move him swiftly. A challenging venture, perhaps, but also a worthy effort, if one is successful.

How then, is this card not describing magical transportation?

Simple - the center focus of this card is not the person being transported, but the conjunction of forces created to armor and convey. Dark and Light, wielded so expertly that no reins are even needed to steer, for the steeds work in tandem. This is a sign of mastery of the Artes of Power - wielding the forces so adroitly that seemingly incompatible Powers are cooperative.

A clue can be found in the sphinxes, as well. Remember, that the Sphinx is the symbol of the Magician and the Riddle. One black (denoting the Unseen and the Dark), and one white (denoting the Seen and the Light); each pulls the Chariot where it must go. Perhaps these beasts are symbols of the two practices of Abjuration - and which steed represents binding, and which would be warding?

The scepter and the crown held by the charioteer shows authority wielded directly, knowledge and power brandished as an enforcement of Will. The armor, however, is like the Chariot itself. The charioteer sees to his own protection first before working wards and bindings of outside purpose. This is good advice for any sorcerer; we must see to our own fastness in all things first.

The absence of the reins also reminds us of our own sorcerous training - do not seek to tell one's subject what to do. Tell it what it is, define it in such a way that it will do what we wish without being told, as a natural result of our sorcery. This is crucial when binding and warding; armor is of no use if it has to be commanded to protect, and a knotted rope is useless if the knot must be watched.

Observe and learn the ways of the Chariot, for the practices of Abjuration are absolutely crucial to most sorcery.

TO ARMOR ONESELF

Round thee draw thy will and breath
Black   White
Left   Right
In   Out
Firm   Stout
Build for life and against death
Black   White
Left   Right
In   Out
Firm   Stout
See thy fastness standing high
Black   White
Left   Right
In   Out
Firm   Stout
Strong and firm in thy mind's eye.

Then draw yoni-lingam charm upon thy breast to avert harm.

THE MOON:
THE SEEMING TRUTH

The Light of the Moon is deceptive and revelatory, showering the land with its power as it hovers between two towers. Beneath the Moon, taking in its light, are a wolf, a hound, and a crayfish. This card is full of symbolism and mystery, which makes sense, as it deals with that subject rather directly.

The arte of Glamoury, also called "seeming" or "illusion," is the practice of manipulating the senses, and the Moon is the card which conveys that concept most acutely. Her ominous and confusing radiance has been blamed for most of human history for all sorts of dangerous behavior. The term "lunacy" speaks of being "moon-touched," and the mad are said to belong to the goddesses of the Moon, most of whom are considered dangerous to humans.

Glamours are one of the more insidious artes of magic. After all, if one can manipulate the senses of a subject, there is very little one cannot make them do. Induce pain, send dreams or nightmares, implant false recollections and conceal memories... the list goes on and on.

There are three beasts upon the card, and likely each represents the kinds of glamour one will cast - glamour to change one's own seeming, glamour to change the seeming of another, and glamour to befuddle the senses of a subject directly. So too, the towers in the background represent the havens we create for ourselves, the mental constructs we design to make ourselves feel safe in this wild world. The Light of the Moon shines all around that landscape, but does not enter the towers, which should also tell us something about glamoury.

Yet, this power needn't be only seen as dangerous and "bad." The Moon sheds Light, after all, and the Light in our cartomantic sorcery tradition is always seen as benign. The power of the Moon is to mirror and reflect the Light, which is seen in the reflective pool incorporated into the card. Deep waters, rippling and untranquil, they reflect the Light even so. So too are glamours born of Light - they reveal unseen things, showcasing the truth in a new way. No glamour is truly a lie; each is designed to not only be built upon a seed of truth, but to grow it in a new way that might have gone unseen.

Under the spell of the Moon's Light, one can converse with a shadow while thinking it is a friend, and in the morning, the words spoken are still true, for all that they derived from our own inner untranquil pool of mystery. That they came not from a person exterior to ourselves does not make the words or feelings less true. Remember that the Light of the Moon transforms all we see into an omen or symbol that we may find its hidden truth within.

A Concealment Spell

Pass	Hand	Over	Face
Moon	Holds	Shade	Done
Into	Dark	Speak	Shape
Eye	Cloak	Words	Gone

THE STAR:
THE INSPIRING LIGHT

The Star is a card depicting a woman pouring water into a rippling pool, and also onto the earth, while great stars shine overhead. Behind her a tree grows. The mysterious nature of this card can cause others to have trouble with its interpretation, and many simply default to the standard association of hope and purity. To be sure, there is some truth to this tradition; the Star does speak of hope. However, all cards can be signs of hope or possibility in the right circumstances. Her real message is about the way she brings hope, and what kind of purity she stands for.

Her nakedness is the first clue. The cards which depict nakedness are not about purity per se, but about rawness and openness. The Strength card also possesses an aspect to it aligned with purity, and yet she is dressed in a white robe. The presence of garb (and also its absence) is a symbol to be interpreted.

Then we have her actions with water, the traditional sign of the emotions and the mysteries of the inner self within the Rider Waite Smith tarots. Like Temperance, she pours water from one place to another, with one foot on the terra firma of our Apparent and empirical reality, and the other in the waters of the unconscious and the Unseen. Unlike Temperance, she pours water out, rather than blending and mixing it. As one of the standards of Temperance is moderation and balancing of one's inner emotional flows, the actions of the Star observed in the same light seem more raw indeed. She pours herself out upon the land, and also pours herself back into the hidden wellspring of her internal psyche.

This card, in all of its cryptic symbolism, is actually a card which teaches about the process of inspiration and persuasion. Its symbols speak directly about the process of bringing someone to understanding.

Bear in mind the card is not called the Naked Woman. It is called the Star, and it is there in the sky that we find our central figure: one great eight-pointed beacon of light, surrounded by six similar ones, and a seventh off from the others. It is the light of the Star which kindles the actions of the woman in the card, and she is our teacher about this magic.

The Star is aloof and distant, representing the Muse this card is often associated with. It speaks of the hunger of artists for their inspiration, and it also speaks of the hunger in all of us to be received, to have our emotions welcomed. This is why the woman is naked - she is raw in her need and in her actions, as one might expect a person needing inspiration or emotional validation to be. That is what this card does; it inspires change in a person's psyche.

The pouring of the waters tells us how one applies a persuasion spell. One can apply one's magic directly into their psychic well of motivation (creating ripples within their psyche), or one can use emotion to grow a greater and more complex sort of compulsion (as one would water the roots of a tree).

The stars in the sky around the central Star tell us what kinds of changes can be inspired, but each of them is a mystery about human behavior. Each star is a different upwelling of motive within the soul. It remains up to the reader to discover what those motives are, but a hint can be found in the positioning of those stars - three each on either side of the great Star, mirroring each other. This implies three levels of motivation within a person, and two kinds of motive born from each. The last star, down on the left, perhaps signifies a completely different kind of motivation, one more personal and less lofty.

A SPELL TO KINDLE INSPIRATION

and

Blazing   *Light*

Heart   *Inspire*   *Mind*

Set   *A'fire*

and

DEATH: THE GREATEST TRANSFORMATION

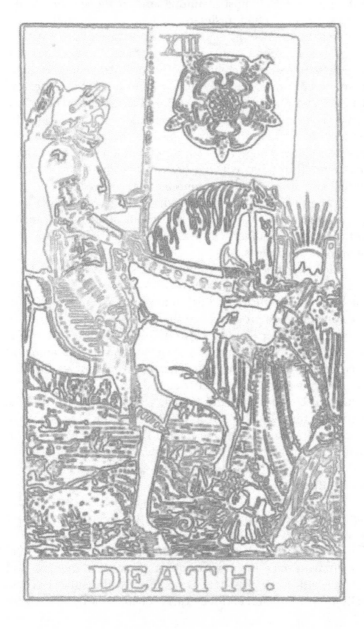

141

The dark armored skeleton upon a white steed, to whom even the priest must give honor - this is the solemn and somewhat grisly figure of Death within the Rider Waite Smith tarot pack. Quite possibly the most daunting and maligned of all the Trumps, Death is often misinterpreted as either more diabolical or more harmless than his nature accurately portrays.

Death is, quite bluntly, not gentle. Many tarot readers will suggest that death is merely a change, and that change is good. These are both true, but they hide a lie in much the same way that the Devil uses truth to lie. Death is a change, to be sure - but change is usually very difficult, especially one meriting the appearance of this card. A change warranting Death's appearance is a change that cannot be avoided, that one cannot walk away from, that will not only change the subject utterly, but will also affect all others connected to the subject.

The symbols in the card illustrate this - the black armor, the elevated position in comparison to all other figures in the card, the dark banner carried in his left hand. Death is triumphant at all times.

However, the other symbols used suggest hope, and one should keep them in mind too. Death's symbol is a white rose, which stands for purity and goodness, and also immortality or longevity. His rose promises that these changes come only when the time is right for them to do so, and that death is part of life. So too, the fact that Death is a skeleton denotes the immortal aspect of our lives, the part of us that is true and unyielding. The priest stands with hands outstretched, in supplication ... or perhaps in benediction. And finally, we see two towers in the distance - the two towers of the Moon, which as we have discussed are symbolic of the mental safe-havens we build for ourselves to protect our psyches from the hazards of the real world. Are we truly safe in those towers? Do we really think that Death cannot enter?

In the end, this card teaches us about Enchantment and magical transformation, which is one of the cornerstones of sorcery. It tells us that change has consequences, and true change transforms all the way to the bone. It shows us that enchantments such as curses or blessings are true changes, and that they affect all they touch, not merely the subject. These spells are triumphant, and they carry a banner of rightness with them, even if the change is unwanted.

There is little more to know about Death, save that it comes to us all. So too, enchantments can and will find all of us, if they are conveyed properly. The "touch of Death" spoken of in myth, which allows the Grim Reaper to cause death simply by touching a subject, is crucial to the effort of enchantment, and yet those who have died under his banner were brought down not by his hand, but by the hooves of his horse. This implies that an enchantment can be conveyed through any appropriate vessel moving under the standard of Death. Indeed, if the priest in the card is intervening (perhaps to spare the child and the maiden), it is likely in the form of sacrifice, another tried-and-true method of undoing or preventing Death (and curses). Martyrdom is the offering of respect to Death while also preserving life for those who are of utmost importance to oneself. This principle conveys itself into all the traditional magicks of spell-breaking and undoing of curses.

A DRAUGHT OF TRANSFORMATION

By cup of venom,
old life ends.
Hand of Death,
Give life again.
  Rise up
  Rise up
  Rise up
  and walk.

Rise up, rise up, and walk.

THE HERMIT:
THE LONELY VISION

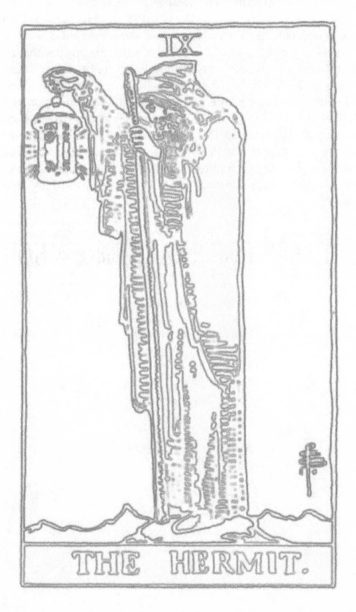

A lone figure overlooks from a mountain peak, robed and carrying lantern and staff. The Hermit represents one who walks alone, who moves apart from the rest of the world for his own reasons. A wanderer and a visionary, his magic is that of True Sight. True vision, the ability to see what is truly there, and not merely what others wish to believe; also known as "common sense," it isn't common at all, and perhaps that is why the Hermit walks alone. True Sight also is a term which refers to psychic perceptive ability, such as clairvoyance or precognition or telepathy. The ability to perceive what is hidden is a necessary talent for most magical practices, as it allows us to "see" magic and the Unseen to a degree, which helps us learn our art.

This card is a relatively easy one to read and learn from; the symbols are obvious and matter-of-fact. The spareness of this card is actually a deeper part of its mystery, however. The lantern represents the Light of seeing, of scrying and psychic perception. His lofty perch assists his seeking. Perspective and a proper vantage is necessary for discovering truth. His staff and robes, however, are a bit harder to understand, and have to do with the mechanism of psychic perception. A psychic ability like true sight requires careful handling, and one must practice with it and master it as one would a weapon, in order to gain any real value from it. Likewise, the robes (as well as the starkness of the environment of the card itself) are a symbol of the mental perspective needed when using one's mystical senses. To see clearly, one must look for truth unvarnished and without pretty or comfortable trappings. Truth is often a barren and harsh thing to learn, and therefore one must divest oneself of fripperies and flattery, approaching not with optimism, but with only a desire for honesty and reality. His robes do nothing to flatter him, and they barely look like they can keep him warm. Truth is always an ordeal, as are gifts of this nature. Often they isolate us and make us unable to interact with the rest of the world properly.

The Hermit is a sign for any who might possess a vision or perspective that is not common within the world. Those of us who sense the Unseen, who see beyond the veils of glamour and expectation, do not find an easy path ahead of us. Still, all magic requires commitment, and True Sight is no different.

A common trick for seeing truly is to touch or gaze upon one's subject as the Hermit does, and allow one's own landscape to go blank as the Hermit's landscape is blank. Then, one can step forward and explore the visions to be seen within the realm of the subject. The trick then is to simply allow the sensations or visions to come, to let the subject's inner world fill in the missing details of one's own blank world.

From there, the use of True Sight is not passive but active. Receptive though it may be, it is an assertive action. A choice to read and look, to sift through memories and future timelines, to shed Light upon the hidden places. The staff symbolizes this act. Often, a reader will create a metaphor representing their willful perusal of the information at hand. For example, one might see oneself flipping through the book of a person's life, or seeing visions in a river of their time.

A SPELL TO SEE THOUGHTS

Touch be Eye, Eye be Light, Light be Road, Road be Sight

Touch		Eye
Eye		Light
Light		Road
Road	Turn	Sight
Sight	the	Touch
Touch	Key	Eye
Eye		Light
Light		Road
Road		Sight

Mind be Door, Door be Wide, Light be Key to See Inside.

JUDGEMENT:
REBIRTH AND RECKONING

As its clearly Biblical imagery might suggest, this card represents judgment of a very specific kind - the kind in which one's actions are called to account, and one is sent on to one's final rewards (or perhaps one's just deserts). Less a card of right and wrong, and more one of consequence and coping, this card leaves no room for negotiation or argument. All Judgement is final here, and refers not to present choices, but past ones already made. It is a card of harvest, and not of sowing seeds.

That being said, its hidden magic is rather interesting; the card refers to Healing, and that side of the card is often overlooked. The bodies of those rising to Gabriel's horn are rejuvenated and revived past all mortal frailty, a clear sign of healing. However, a lesser noted sign can be found in the banner on the trumpet. The red cross, commonly thought to be a depiction of the St. George Cross, is also a common symbol for healing and medical services, and has been known since 1859 for just that purpose. So too, the archangel Gabriel is said to be a messenger, but of good news.

The Healing artes are not merely arts of renewal, however - and this card shows the rather grim aspect of healing as well as the more friendly side. One can just as easily use one's healing power to wither or harm, and often some of the more nasty "curses" cast upon a person may have deleterious effects based on withering magic. The trumpet wielded by Gabriel is often called the Trump of Doom, and it holds no power to save or offer second chances. When it is heard, those on the side of the angels rise to meet them, and for the others, well... the Devil takes his due.

That being said, the card comes as a herald of freedom and hope, a sign of renewal and new vitality. There are no souls on this card who do not rise, and the card is a good omen. That, in general, is the true purpose of the magic of Healing; once it is done, it returns all to rightness and balance again, and the slate is wiped clean.

When performing healing upon a subject, one must remember to mind the state of the subject's own balance before meddling. Their bodies are a reflection of their own Light and its actions, and one must take care to rectify any unbalancing factors before activating healing forces. After all, leaving a knife or arrow within someone's body and healing around it is unlikely to solve much of their problem.

A simple order of operations when healing:

- Learn as much as you can about the problem or problems, and be prepared to address those problems.

- Like Gabriel's horn, calm the subject and help them release their panic first before beginning to heal.

Heal from the root, not the tip. Do not simply treat symptoms; work on solving the most crucial problem first.

- Follow up with them after it is over; give them something to do and a new destiny to walk into.

And always remember: a magician is not a doctor, and legally we cannot practice medicine without a license. Never try to take the place of a doctor's advice.

A SPELL FOR HEALING

Body mind and spirit mend.
Breath and blood
Flesh and bone
Cross the heart to thwart the end.
Breath and blood
Flesh and bone
Succor and salvation send.

JUSTICE:
A PRECISE BALANCE

The final arbiter in the tarot deck, Justice holds sway over all decisions of right and wrong. However, the tarot are not confined to any legal or religious doctrine of morality - they see from a position of balance and greater purpose. The great pillars on either side of the throned figure are very similar to those depicted in the Hierophant card, and thus to the pillars of the High Priestess. In this card, they denote boundaries and confines - limitations to action.

This is further expanded upon by the square in the center of her crown; squares are signs of safety and boundary. The brooch which acts as her cloak clasp also is a square, with a circle in the middle, a symbol denoting the four elements of nature enforcing an inner unity and perfection. This is the true message of the Justice card - not of legal squabbles or church dogma, but that of natural balance and harmony with a greater design.

Fitting, it would seem, that the arte taught by this card is that of weather working (which we will also call "elementalism") - the manipulation of the balances of nature to create desired environmental effects, such as rain or wind or temperature change. This magic can be used to rein in the natural elements (like preventing a fire from consuming one's home), and also pushing them out of balance. However, the magicks used to manipulate nature's balance are often considered advanced by most traditions, as they can go drastically wrong. In the tarot card depicted here, Justice is not blind as she is often portrayed to be in courtrooms. She uses her eyes, and acts upon her own wisdom and common sense. The scales show the careful weighing of her decisions, and the sword shows the possible outcome of imbalance.

Weather magic is actually a simple process, if one is not impatient or self-centered. The moving of nature's balances to provide a safer or healthier environment is a relatively easy spell. The harnessing of the weather to create dramatic effects or the use of the elements to cause violent change are not as simple, nor as advisable. The best outcome of such a spell is that it will not work. Trying to fling fire or summon lightning upon command is only really valued by those with a mind for dramatics and posturing, as one can just as easily frighten or destroy opposition without all the flash and special effects.

Indeed, the pursuit of such magic is not wise. After all, in order to have lightning, you must first have the proper circumstances for it (such as a thunderstorm), and those come with their own problems. Fire does not come from nothing - it must be stimulated, and it must be fed.

In the end, it is best to work with the cycles and currents of nature, rather than to try to wrest control of them for the flattering of one's ego. That being said, weather spells are no different from any other magic. Simply craft an image or action which mirrors the change in the weather, and use the Five Practices to enact one's design.

A CHARM FOR CALLING WIND

Wake
Lord
From
Sleep so Still
By   *By*
My   *Will My*   *Will*

To Calm the Breeze

Sleep
Friend
And
Rest Again
Wind   *Wind*
Now   *Wane*   *Now*   *Wane*

THE FOOL'S JOURNEY
AND THE SPELL OF SEEKING

As we have mentioned, some traditions practice a spread known as the Fool's Journey - a laying of the Trumps in three "roads" of seven (or two "roads" of eleven, a variant which we won't be discussing in this book), with a single card left out to represent the querent. This spread is simply a divination for some - designed to show them where they are on their great journey, sort of like spreading one's fairy tale or myth cycle out in front of one. It allows us to get a basic idea of where we're going and what challenges await us along the way.

However, our practice of Cartomantic Sorcery uses this spread for more than a simple laying of Trumps. The pattern of three rows of seven, with one left over, is of great significance to us in our practice. It refers to the three standard kinds of Mediums (and the elusive fourth kind, the Ephemera), and allows us to focus on our journey of discovery as sorcerers, and what wisdom these three paths have to show us as individuals. Make no mistake, sorcerers are fiercely independent creatures, and we like to work with our magic in individualistic ways.

In addition to the divinatory practice described above, this particular spread holds special significance the first time a practitioner of this book's tradition uses it. It acts as a rite of dedication to the powers of Cartomantic Sorcery. By laying the cards, we lay the path before us; by choosing a significator, we place our feet upon the path. Once we begin doing that, we have begun to walk.

The following short ritual will describe in detail the steps of this spread as both dedication and divination. It is recommended that a practitioner of the sorcery described in this book do this ritual once a year, beginning right after the performance of the Rite of the Adytum. Should one ever find themselves lapsing in their practice, a good way to begin again is to lay this spread; one needn't reconsecrate the tools, as magic doesn't just go away. This ceremony and spread can be performed for others, either as a simple divination or a full dedication, but dedication requires that they have performed the Rite of the Adytum.

COMMENCING THE JOURNEY

Begin by choosing a Significator for the querent (which we will assume is yourself for now), in whatever manner you choose. Some prefer to choose a card based on their birth information (astrological and numerological correspondences are common methods of doing this). Some will prefer to simply select based on their pre-determined preference, and others will simply draw randomly.

Once the card is chosen, look at it closely. By our selection, this card has become our Guide. It will act as an attending blessing upon us (based on its nature), and it will also function as a lens through which we can Seek wisdom and understanding. By comparing our chosen Significator's theme with the card we are currently working through on the roads (and then comparing that to our current inner and outer environment), we can learn what it is the cards are trying to teach us.

After we have chosen our card and considered its purpose and theme as our Guide, we can move forward into the reading itself. Each path has an overlaying theme in and of itself, which we will discuss on the next page. However, each column within the spread has special significance in and of itself, and we will discuss that in the following pages as well.

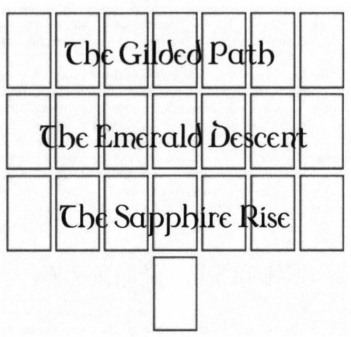

The three "roads" in the Fool's Journey deal with the three layers of the world around us: personal, interpersonal, and transpersonal. The fourth layer, the ephemeral, is seen through the moving of the Guide, who represents the Fool's Dog in this particular spread, guiding us through the cards and advising us.

As sorcerers, it is important to learn these three roads - naturally so that we can observe and utilize appropriate Mediums in our sorcery, but also so that we can observe reality as it truly is, and not merely delude ourselves into seeing it as we want it to be. One cannot change what one cannot perceive in any useful way.

The three roads are as follows:

I.   The Gilded Path: the way of the personal, and mastering one's inherent nature and gifts, pertaining to indwelling qualities.

II.   The Emerald Descent: the way of the interpersonal, and mastering the powers and magicks of one's environment, pertaining to external relational subjects.

III.   The Sapphire Rise: the way of the transpersonal, wherein one aligns with the extradimensional and transcendent, pertaining to larger-picture manifestations and entities.

The three roads are aspects to every initiation, and the spread can act as a road map through our own journey, no matter which kind of initiations we are currently working upon.

They also are roads by which one can understand the manifold ways Light moves through and shapes the Dark, creating Mediums out of seemingly ordinary circumstances. This can be seen in the sevenfold process of each card in a road, and how they correspond.

As previously mentioned, the seven steps in each road are all linked. They are described as follows:

1.   The Step of Dominion, the assertion of one's Will and design

2.   The Step of Departure, the exit from the illusion into the heart of Light

3.   The Step of Fascination, the beckoning of the subject to the Light

4.   The Step of Mandate, the enactment of the change upon that which is within one's Umbra

5.   The Step of Communion, the integration of the Light's new design with one's consciousness

6.   The Step of Consequence, the acceptance of the price of Light's work

7.   The Step of Harmony, the committing of all forces

to design in balance

These steps can be seen as both a seven-step ritual, but they can also be seen as seven different methods of understanding Mediums within their sphere of Manifestation. For example, the first step of Affirmation is aligned with the Magician in the personal sphere, Strength in the environmental, and the Devil in the transcendental. Each of these is an explanation of the nature of a Medium, and also a method of unleashing the Light within a Medium for mystical purposes. The theme of each step on the road can be further expressed thus:

1.   The Magician, the Step of Personal and Inner Dominion

2.   The High Priestess, the Step of Personal and Inner Departure

3.   The Empress, the Step of Personal and Inner Fascination

4.   The Emperor, the Step of Personal and Inner Mandate

5.   The Hierophant, the Step of Personal and Inner Communion

6.   The Lovers, the Step of Personal and Inner Consequence

7.   The Chariot, the Step of Personal and Inner Harmony

8.   Strength, the Step of Interpersonal and Environmental Dominion

9.   The Hermit, the Step of Interpersonal and Environmental Departure

10.   The Wheel of Fortune, the Step of Interpersonal and Environmental Fascination

11.   Justice, the Step of Interpersonal and Environmental Mandate

12.   The Hanged Man, the Step of Interpersonal and Environmental Communion

13.   Death, the Step of Interpersonal and Environmental Consequence

14.   Temperance, the Step of Interpersonal and Environmental Harmony

15.   The Devil, the Step of Transpersonal and Transcendent Dominion
16.   The Tower, the Step of Transpersonal and Transcendent Departure
17.   The Star, the Step of Transpersonal and Transcendent Fascination
18.   The Moon, the Step of Transpersonal and Transcendent Mandate
19.   The Sun, the Step of Transpersonal and Transcendent Communion
20.   Judgement, the Step of Transpersonal and Transcendent Consequence
21.   The World, the Step of Transpersonal and Transcendent Harmony

Once one has laid out all the cards, and begun to analyze each step on each path, one may write down the layout and use it in the future as a roadmap through one's Journey. Traditionally, the Journey takes either 40 days and nights (reflecting the Biblical number of ordeal) or a year and one month (associated with the number of Lesser Arcana in the deck, with some days left over to represent the Trump one has chosen as Guide, and this is commonly associated more with traditional 52-card "poker" decks). These are considered very loose time-lines, as there is no true time limit on one's mystical development. Nevertheless, they should give one an idea of how long and involved this ritual can be.

Following the guidance of the Trumps, one uses the Fool's Journey to master each of the Steps of the three Roads for one's own use, and to be changed in turn by each of them. If one has the Devil in the position of the Step of Interpersonal Mandate (the position aligned with Justice), and one has chosen the Star as one's Guide, then one must learn and then utilize Interpersonal Mandate to master the Devil's mystery (which we know as the Light of Divination), with the Star providing aid through guiding omens of its nature.

There is no wrong way to do this rite, nor to interpret this reading, save by giving up and allowing oneself to remain in ignorance. By the very contemplation of these concepts, one unlocks hidden pathways in oneself and in the world for oneself.

Thus is the initiation accomplished even if one's answers are vastly different from those of others doing the same work.

Should one desire to use this spread in the future as a predictive method, one can simply choose a Significator, shuffle it in with all the other Trumps, and then lay the Trumps into the pattern of the Three Roads. The card left over is laid over the Significator in the spread (unless of course one has managed to select their Significator), and that will tell one where in the Journey one already is at. If the Significator is the leftover card, one has finished a Journey and has yet to begin another.

Divination with this spread can also be easily done by associating the cards with the Trump whose position they hold. If the Empress is in the Star's position that may imply that the Empress' power of love and fortune resides around the idea of inspiration and hope.

In any case, the Journey spread is this book's solution for the learning of one's own magic. Once we have learned our own magic, we can begin to learn the magic within the cards themselves, and thereby find the mastery we desire.

From here we will enter into the second half of this book, which might more appropriately be considered a spellbook. As these first sections are designed around explaining the theory of magic and how one becomes a cartomantic sorcerer, the next area is intended to depict spells of various kinds, which one can perform by using the cards themselves. In addition will be several appendices of basic non-cartomantic magic which one can use to design things like potions and dusts, and a number of helpful spreads for simple divination.

A reminder: all spreads in this book can be used for divination as they are, although their purposes are often not strictly divinatory. Feel free to use this book to your own specifications as you please.

And now, on to the spells!

CHAPTER FOUR: THE BOOK OF COUNTED IMAGES

BEING A COMPLETE COLLECTION OF SPELLS, POTIONS AND RITES FOR ALL OCCASIONS OF CARTOMANTIC SORCERY

THE MAGIC CIRCLE

Fourfold the Paths of Mastery,
the lessons we must learn,
the Lights of wisdom and Ordeal,
the admonition stern.

Sixfold be the Talisman,
the Lights of magic's birth -
by these, the Light is cozened
from each Medium of worth.

Twelvefold the Arts of Sorcery,
Circl'd magicks we create,
Like unto the signs of Zodiac,
all Light we fascinate.

First Four, then Six, then Dozen lay,
from center moving out,
then Circle's incantation say,
to cast this spell about.

With this Circle, I entwine,
all Light and Dark to my design.
By the Cross and Charm and Wheel, this be
a haven for my sorcery.

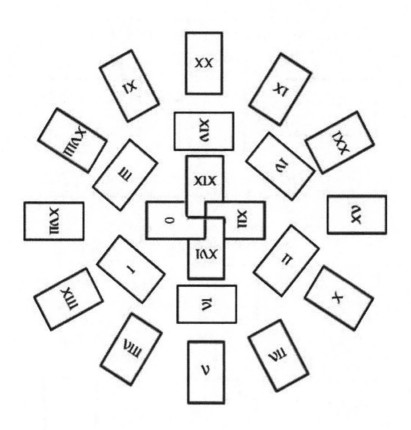

ThE MΔKING OF SPELLS

A spread's a spell, a weaving of the Light;
its pattern shapes the Darkness with thy might.

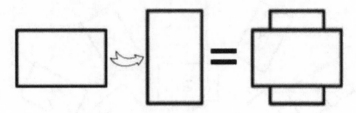

One card choose first, thy subject Signify.
Then cross and claim with thy supremacy.

Then four around, in perfect compass lie,
the other Practices of Sorcery.

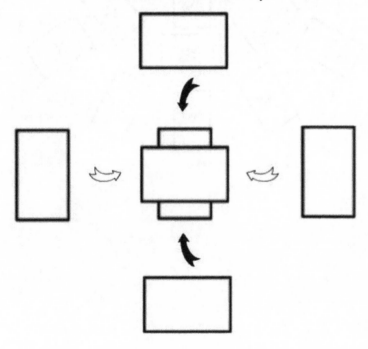

By Triangle of Art, do ye devise
The virtue in each card, and bid it rise.
From each of these, choose emblems pictured there,
to act as potent Medium of care.

Then weave together all the cards as one,
and touch and speak each card to send its Light.
To finish, speak forth thy incantation,
then speak "So Mote It Be" to bind it tight.

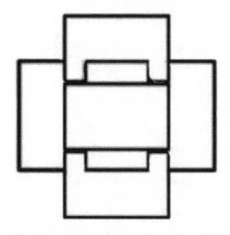

Say:

By Light from (Northern symbol) I bespeak thy Body,
By Light from (Southern symbol) I break thy Bond,
By Light from (Western symbol) I bind thy Heart,
By Light from (Eastern symbol) I bend thy Face,
Thou I name and thou I frame,
Thou art (name from the cross card) as I proclaim!
SO MOTE IT BE!

S. Rune Emerson

The Calling of the Jack

A mage's work is never finished,
and oft in sorcery,
when we do find ourselves diminished
in our capacity,
'tis wise to call upon some aid,
a wight with whom a Pact is made,
A stalwart sort who'll do as bade,
with true tenacity.

Tis thus we weave this calling rite -
to beckon unto such a sprite
and through attention thus invite
familiarity.

The first step is, if we'd behold
the spirit we beseech -
We conjure it with Name threefold:
a card we lay for each.
One for the spoken Name it rides
One for the secret Name it hides
And one for the sigil Name which guides,
and which extends its reach.

These three place in the center, laid
in hexagonal way.
Then round the rest a cross is made -
four crosses ye shall lay.

The East for its Perspective.
The South for its Puissance.

The West for its Demeanor.
The North for its Countenance.

Then over these, lay hands and say
the following, the charm to lay:

Say:
Spirit to Spirit,
I summon ye -
By threefold Name
of Sorcery.
One to speak,
One to see,
One to keep in secrecy.
(Spirit's spoken name), come to me.

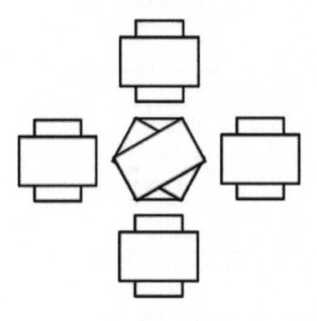

S. Rune Emerson

THE KNIGHT'S VIGIL

The road is long,
the nights are longer,
and challenges
get only stronger.

They say that forewarned
is forearmed.
With knowledge, ye
are ever charmed.

Draw three cards each
for four directions
as in compass
predilection.

Lay them out
as trine inverted,
and each shall be
a trial subverted.

Armor first, the situation
lays the trial's firm foundation.
Right the sword to challenge hard,
and Left the shield, to save and ward.

Each triad is a trial's sigil,
each a Knight holding a vigil.

East is Dawn, new fate arriving.
South is Noon, endeavors thriving.
West is Dusk, and hearts departing,
and North is Midnight and evil's thwarting.

Over these, raise weapon hand,
and speak this spell as a command -

Say:

One to guard,
One to guide,
One to bid,
and one to bide.

I dedicate my day to thee -
Knights of the Cross,
Attend to me!

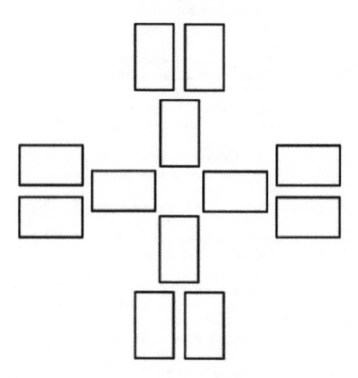

The Queen's Mirror

Legend tells of a mirror tall,
which hung upon a royal wall.
When asked directly and correctly,
it answered truth to one and all.

This mirror true, thy cards can show,
and answers truthful ye may know.
Yet take care what seeds ye sow -
a foolish wish may bring ye woe.

A card for ye, at bottom place -
to show your true and proper face.

A card for your reflection clear,
where question's answer shall appear.

Around it lay four cards to frame
and each with purpose and with name -

The Right for words to give thee Faith,
the Left to give thee Fear,
the Bottom for thy dearest Hope,
and the Top for what's Unclear.
Connect each card with one card more,
creating yet another four -

Faith and Hope
breed Wish come true,
Hope and Fear
breed Payments due,

Fear and Doubt
bring Doom to bear,
but Doubt and Faith

hold Anchors there.
The final cards are formed from thee -

advise yourself by questions three.
One card for Youth, and one for Age,
and Death which makes of all a sage.

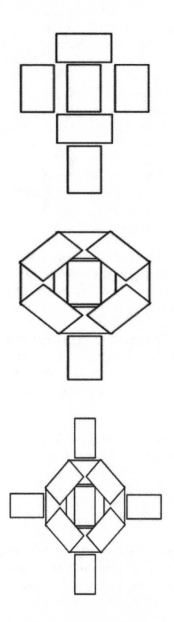

The Scepter of Sovereignty

Light upon thy being
casts a shadow 'cross the land.
All who walk within thy Umbra
are subject to thy command.

Loyal to thy purpose,
like a liegeman to a lord,
they count upon thy sovereignty,
to vanquish aught untoward.

Yet remember, as with all things,
this protection bears a cost.
Any dwelling in thy bower
must obey thee or be lost.

First choose Significator,
to denote thy subject clear,
then lay cross'd their card another,
to command them to appear.

Then around them like a flower,
with its petals blooming wide,
lay six cards to tell their story -
each a nuance to confide.

Say:
Word is bond and will is light,
I summon ye into my sight.
Stand forth and speak,
that I shall hear,
and to my oath,
all shall adhere!

Then six more cards lay beneath,
each facing up and unto thee.
These are dictums ye may issue,
each an edict or decree.

Take up each of these commandments,
and upon a circled card,
each is laid as intercession,
bound by weight of thy regard.

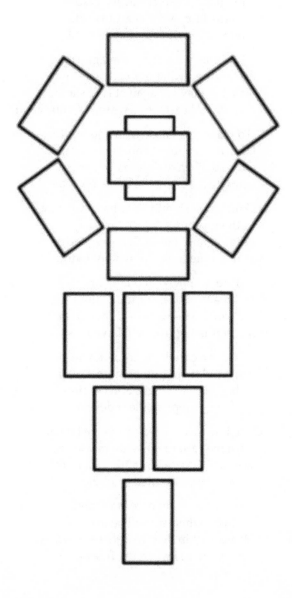

ᚦO BESPEAK A HEARᚦ

Trump to pip to courtly face,
thy deck possesses every grace -
a card for every heart to beat,
no matter who or what ye meet.

'Tis thus we work our magic so,
that all heed what our cards bestow.
For what may yet against thee stand,
when 'round their heart ye've wrapped your hand?

To make this magic firm and hard,
Bid that thy subject choose their card.
Once they have done as ye design,
Their fate is sealed, their heart is thine.

Yet know that should their hand yet stay,
there yet may be another way.
If they choose not as they are bidden,
use other methods known but hidden.

Fate cannot be avoided, pray -
feel free to choose for them, thy way.
Be warned, however - if they stray
from their new card, ye'll have no sway.

Only a card by their own will
can bind them firm enough to still
their future choices and confine
them to a permanent design.

Once into card their heart ye've taken,
Turn the card to make them waken.
Like the Hanged Man, they shall see,
and be committed unto thee.

No incantation here is needed -
all you whisper shall be heeded.
Heard within their heart's recesses,
they are a slave to thy finesses.

S. Rune Emerson

TO CONJURE AN OMEN

When the world will give no aid,
Let the tarot be your guide.
Cut the cards into two piles,
and in each hand, weigh either side.

Left hand holds your heart and need,
right hand holds the world's weight.
Say this spell, and they will heed,
and offer you a sign of Fate.

Say:
Card to card, by heart of Light,
shift the scales from wrong to right.
Before the Day gives way to Night,
Bring a sign into my sight.

From each pile, a card you lay,
the right above, the left below.
In cruciform, the spell shall play
and from the cards, a sign bestow.

Yet ware ye - omens are no toy,
each is a key unto a door.
If ye follow not Fate's ploy,
Fortune may not aid ye more.

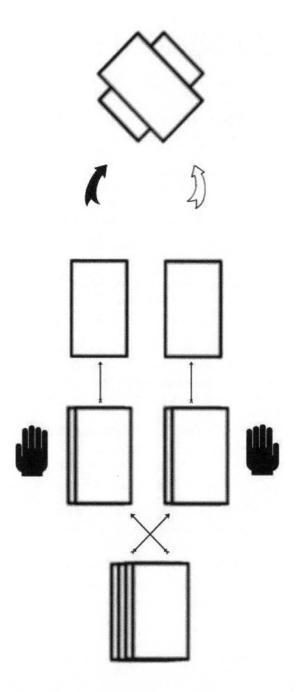

TO SEE FROM AFAR

In ancient times, a trick called "scrying"
oft was used for distance-spying.
With this spell, your senses cast
to future, present, or to past.

Begin by drawing into view
a tarot which will stand for you.
Then just above, one more shall lie,
to show the subject you would scry.

Say:
Eye of magic, fly from me,
and gaze upon what I would see.
Be it far or be it near,
Show it as if it were here.

Close eyes, and let your sight's regard
see out from the first tarot card.
Gaze up and look upon your face,
then close the eye, and change your place.

From second card, look forth and peek,
and once again, surroundings seek.
Then turn within the card, and send
your senses to where you intend.

Within the card, possess the sky,
if you from overhead would spy.
Yet if up close you'd look and scry,
then borrow creature's ear and eye.

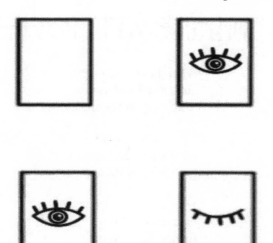

S. Rune Emerson

TO COMMUNE WITH ANOTHER

When heart and eye
are joined and see,
a true rapport is born.

If ye would read
what's written there
and share thine without scorn,

Draw two cards from
a deck entire,
with one for each of ye,

And join them in
a heart's design,
and speak thus, openly:

Say:
Heart to heart,
eye to eye,
we shall see
beyond all lie.
Truth and wisdom
we do share,
that Light may stand
against despair.

Thereafter
when the two are near,
shall each know other's heart.

And this shall last
till both are done
and hearts decide to part.

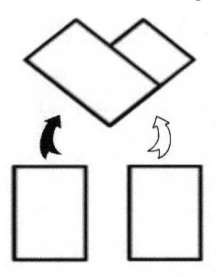

S. Rune Emerson

TO CONCEAL A SECRET

If ye'd keep thy secrets hidden,
lay the cards in following style.
Cut the deck in twain as bidden,
then flip the top of the rightmost pile.

This card shows what you'd conceal -
the significator needed.
Next a card from left pile steal -
face down, over the other seated.

Say:
Left hand hides what right hand shows -
what I conceal, no other knows.

So long as left card covers right,
magic ever blinds their sight.

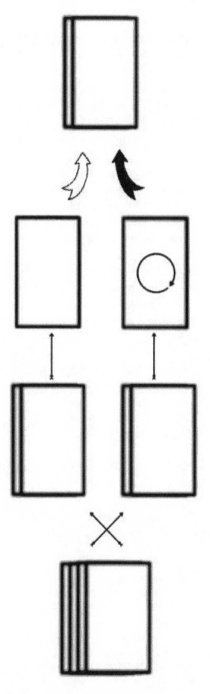

TO ENSURE AN ADVANTAGE

The world can often be unfair,
and skill may not be all you need.
If others deal with ye unsquare,
this spell can help ye plant a seed.

Take three cards from your deck and lay
them in a hexagonal way.
One for luck,
One for wit,
One for aid in all you say.

Leave these cards upon a place
where sun and moon may faintly shine.
And over each card you bespeak
this incantation, all in rhyme.

Say:
Sun and Moon and Stars unite
and grant to me your braided Light.
What skill is mine
do now entwine,
to bless my working and my right.

Then cloak the cards from other's vision,
that they may not invest derision.

By thy work, it shall be plain -
against all odds, thy skill shall reign.

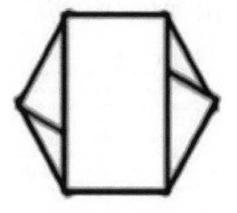

ŦO OPEN ŦĦE WAỾ

When opportunity must knock,
but options forward can't be found,
this spell can make a door unlock,
or form a bridging path around.

First draw a card to signify
thyself in thy predicament,
then draw two more and crossed, ply
them as a clear impediment.

Then speak this spell, as if to chide,
and turn the cards to either side:

Say:
Left hand beckons,
right hand guards.
Password opens ways and wards.

Then a secret word unknown
do whisper where the cards are thrown.
Go forth unto thy life and walk,
and speak this word to move the block.

Be warned, this magic will not last -
use it once and then recast.

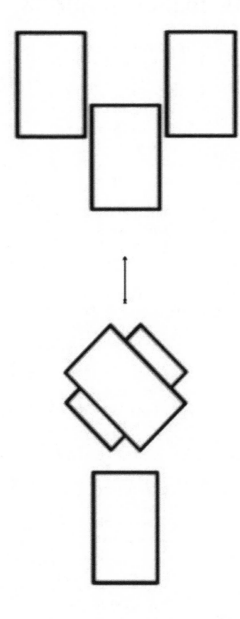

TO INDUCE A HUMOR

When spirits are low
and sadness holds sway,
a little magic
can go a long way.

Use this charm
to turn the tide
and bring a better
mood to bide.

Draw three cards
from thy pack -
a singer each
to turn ill back.

Lay them in
the pattern shown
then speak this spell
to them alone:

Say:
Singers three I call to me,
from misty western isle.
One named Mirth,
One named Birth,
and one named Hopeful Smile.

Place each card
in hidden spaces
far from people's
eyes and faces.

While they dwell
within the spell,
its magic shall
assist them well.

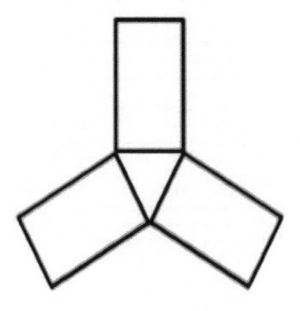

To Send a Message

Often in our lives, we find
that others do not listen well.
If ye discover such a mind,
consider this bespeaking spell.

Draw one card as significator
for the one whose ears disdain,
then cross them with another card
which shows the reason ye complain.

Then draw a third like dagger's blade,
and over crossed hilt and bar,
place it as thy message laid
and speak this spell from where you are.

Say:
Sharp the blade
and true the sword,
this my message and my word.
Whether ye would heed or not,
Feel my blade in every thought.

Ware - some wisdom is not plain.
If they must learn, there may be pain.

Yet rest assured, this spell's design
is geared for missives not malign.
No need for worry or alarm -
though there be pain, it shall not harm.

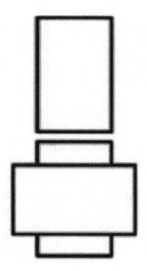

To Sequester Beyond Time

To preserve what ye do treasure
and hold priceless beyond measure,
lay these cards as witching wards
to set aside and await your leisure.

One for what you'd squirrel away,
and then one o'er its bottom lay,
then cap the spread upon the head
with third atop the whole array.

The lower card denotes the vault
while the top's a ward to halt,
and intertwined, they keep confined
thy treasure safe from all assault.

Then final card lay o'er the three,
and turn'd to 180 degree,
a lock is made, and charm is laid,
and none shall take this thing from thee.

To formalize the spell in strength,
the incantation speak at length.

Say:
Magic bind,
Magic mind -
thus entwined,
None shall find.

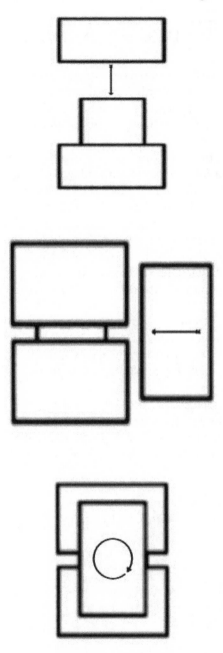

S. Rune Emerson

TO BLESS A BOND

Be they formed of strong affection,
luck, or mutual direction,
life is full of ties which bind,
a fact of life that's oft-maligned.

Yet, though some ties are viewed askance,
and frowned upon with sideways glance,
there are some bonds which lift us high,
and through their virtue dignify.

'Tis these entwinements we would charm,
and sanctify against all harm.
Lay forth these cards if ye'd convey
a marriage free from trouble's sway.

In squaring pattern, lay ye four
and bring in left and right to bless -
these two are warded evermore,
with top and bottom to witness.

Speak the words as spell of Light,
and let the bond be forged in might.
As ye do speak, now Dark must heed
and by their bond, thy friends are freed.

Say:
Witnessed by Heaven,
Witnessed by Earth.
None may sever -
Bound forever.

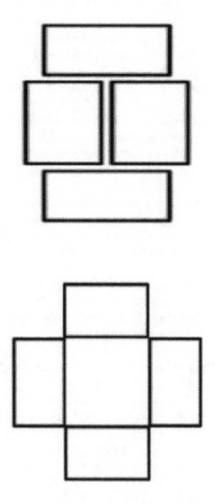

S. Rune Emerson

TO CAUSE REFLECTION

Hearts are funny things -
they make apologies but rarely.
What they feel is what they feel,
and they command our thoughts unfairly.

If we'd seek a path of wisdom,
often we must refuge take,
and in solitude unburden
that our mental fog may break.

Should we be so heavy weighted
by unquiet heart and mind,
use this method as a haven
to reflect and thus unwind.

Into equal piles approximate
four times cut the deck and lay.
Then arranged in diamond shape, create
a space to steal away.

Flip the top four cards and name them right,
and bid them aid and interdict.
Thus are ye protected quite
until thy heart has gained new sight.

Say:
Walls for birth
and walls for life
and walls for ending to all strife.
Walls for truth and peace of mind,
walls I raise, myself to find.

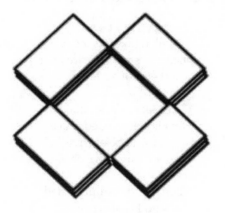

S. Rune Emerson

TO WARD REPOSE

Sleep is a blessing
which takes us away
when our struggles are over
at end of each day.

Oft taken for granted
this much-needed grace
can well be elusive,
and we must give chase.

When health is diminished,
and body is tired
let this be the magic
when rest is desired.

Choose card for the weary,
and lay them supine.
Then three lay beneath
as a place to recline.

Each of these is a sword -
an offense to one's peace.
With this spell ye shall tame them
that trouble shall cease.

Speak the following charm,
and name each, one by one.
Then turn each facing down again
that spell be done.

Say:
Blades within (touch the left)
and blades without (touch the right)
blade of mine (touch the center)
turn blades about (flip each face down).

From now until this one would rise,
these blades defend their resting eyes.

Now turn the sleeper's
card face in,
that blessed slumber
they may win.

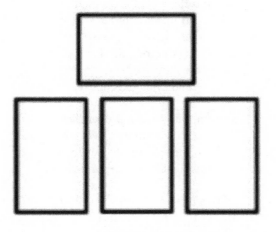

S. Rune Emerson

ȚO PEȚIȚION WINȚER

Far to the North,
where the Star shines bright
and the world is dressed
in rippling lights,
there stands a House
beyond our sight -
the House of Winter
and Silent Night.

From this place, a power flies
invisible to mortal eyes.
It brings a coldness to our lives
as chill as death, as sharp as knives.

If this privation you would call
and bring it from behind its wall,
craft first an arch from five cards tall,
with fifth as Star o'er-seeing all.

Then turn the Star as knob to door
and through the gateway ye implore.
Let thy petition thusly soar,
then close the gate and say no more.

Say:
By dark of night and steadfast star
I call the snows from where they are.
Across the land and through the air,
I grant to them my solemn prayer.

(speak your concern and seek aid from Winter)

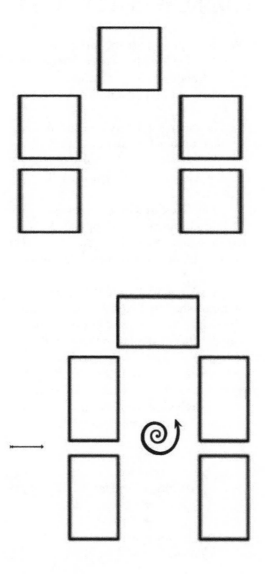

TO BREW A TEMPEST

When life goes stagnant and unclean,
and fouled are places once-serene,
tranquility is no solution
to expel and oust pollution.

When man's wit defy and spurn,
then unto nature shall we turn!
Know ye this - all is not lost!
Let the land be tempest-tossed!

Lay five cards in pentagon -
to each a purpose be appraised.
Then turn each toward where troubles spawn,
and set them free, that hell be raised!

Speak this spell unto the cards
that they shall fly like witching wards.
The winds and rains and sky and land
against the ill shall turn their hand.

Yet know that once the storm is brought,
then none are safe from what ye've wrought,
save ye whose power raised it high -
around ye, calm shall find its eye.

Say:
One, Two,
Three, Four, Five.
Weep and wail the winds alive.
Five, Four,
Three, Two, One,
Hell shall reign till bane be gone!

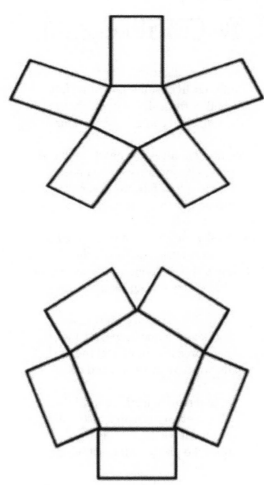

TO CONJURE RAIN

They say it's true for one and all:
into our lives some rain must fall.
Whether from sky or our own eye,
the rain shall come, however small.

One thing is sure - the heart can bleed,
and to its sorrow we must heed.
Yet, though unfair, 'tis best to care,
for pain like this is born from need.

When sky must darken black like lead,
to thus enshroud us overhead
and clouds should loom like ships of doom,
which carry off our blessed dead,

Lay five cards in a line across,
and let each one bespeak a loss.
Then three invert, to heal the hurt
and wash away debris and dross.

Yet two remain upright and filled,
that memory remains instilled
in what we do, for it is true -
upon the past we all must build.

Say:
Hearts weep,
skies weep,
rain falls,
I sleep.

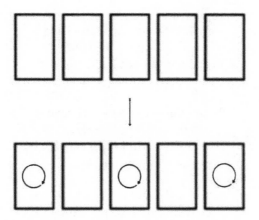

TO TURN THE WINDS

North and South, West and East,
from high above the land,
Winds are summoned and released
by Nature's living hand.

Round the globe in swifter time
than birds can ever fly,
winds cavort and caper forth,
unseen across the sky.

Clever, sly, and full of tricks,
the winds are rarely caught,
and effortlessly change our fates
with ne'er a second thought.

A sorcerer of good virtue
will thus seek to befriend
the winds above, that they be true,
and not bring forth his end.

If ye succeed in winning aid,
this charm of cards for ye is made -
in pattern thus let five be laid,
then favors ask, and price be paid.

Say:
*Lay them low
to raise them high.
Brother, blow
and turn the sky!*

Yet mark ye this -
if ye've not sought
and gained their aid,
then cast it not!

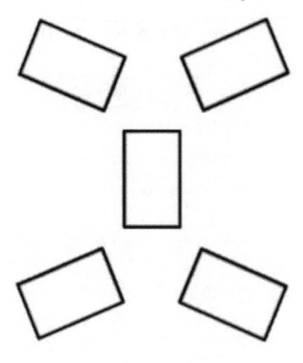

THE SCALES OF GAIN

When luck and odds against ye stack,
and all that you perceive is lack,
remember well this little spell
that ledger shift from red to black.

Draw one card to significate,
and two on either side.
As horizontal scales of Fate,
the two shall now abide.

Then lay three cards upon the right,
face down to stand as coin.
From right to left move each and
turn each up, the spell to join.

As each is turned to face us,
count each blessing you acquire.
Then the three of these
a magic make
to charm thy Fate entire.
Then carry these three cards with you,
in truth or effigy.
Their magic shall their gift imbue
through their proximity.

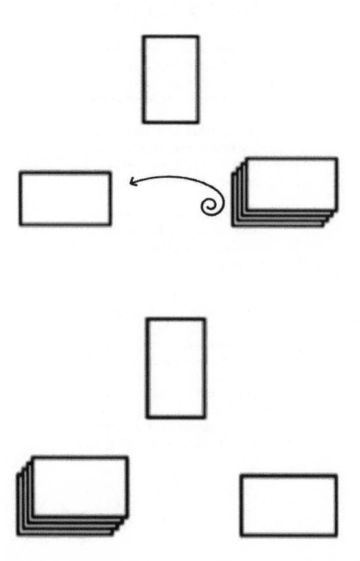

The Red Carpet

If we would walk free of aggression
and be free from intercession,
we must part the gathered crowd
with carpet red and head unbowed.

Use this enchantment to thy path
to keep thee free of other's wrath.
Exalted to thy truest station,
all shall part in admiration.

Lay ye down three piles of two -
in line before thee they accrue.
Then separate to either side
that they as witnesses may bide.

Say:
Left and right, like Moses' art
my path of red decree.
The crowd to either side shall part
and all give way to me.

Yet know this and be ye wary -
spells like these are temporary.
Dawn or Noon or Dusk or Night,
the next threshold shall end its might.

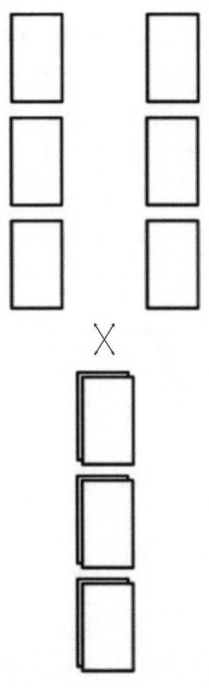

TO DRAW WAYWARD SOULS

Is object parted far from thee?
Have thieves purloined thy property?
Do lovers stray and stroll away?
This spell restores their loyalty.

Lay six cards in a broken line -
each one a memory.
Then up and down the path refine
to bring them back to thee.

Then speak the spell and turn each card
from far away unto thee toward.
Speak words of spell and be it done -
And thus thy summoning's begun.

A note - this spell can take correction
to send things away.
If ye'd an alternate direction,
Point the spread that way.

Then turn the cards from near to far
and let it go from where ye are -
unto thy destination send them;
there thy subject's actions bend them.

Say:
*Road be straight
and path be clear -
unto thy feet
the way appear.*

*Step by step
I bid and bide.
Till heart and heart
be side by side.*

In six day's time,
if ne'er a sign
of them ye've seen,
their heart's not thine.

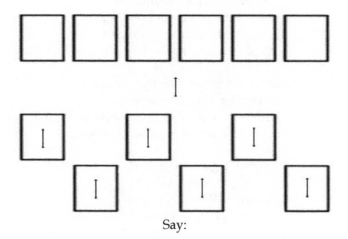

Say:

S. Rune Emerson

TO TRAVEL IN SAFETY

If into Darkness ye must walk,
where danger lives and peril stalks,
Precaution we can ill afford
to go without - a traveling ward.

Lay card for thee, and then across'd,
a card of coin, to pay the cost.
Then four below thee lay as shown,
and each be named, the charm to own.

A card to guide with light to see,
A card to open like a key.
A card to hide, that foes be blind,
and one to guard with watchful mind.

When cards are laid, thy task must be
to pay the price accorded thee.
Then, over thine intended steed,
do whisper words, to seal the deed.

Yet take precaution - share ye never
words to ward thy carriage clever.
If thy names another claims,
their charm from thee be lost forever.

Say:
Farrier,
Carrier,
Here to there.
Four to shoe the steed.
One to ward and one to guard
One to hold and one to heed!

(whisper the names)
Waken to my will!

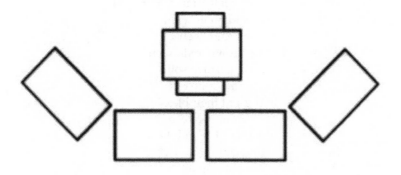

ꝼO PLⱯNꝼ Ɐ ꞅEEꝺ

Some spells start small
and go unseen,
concealed beneath
the brown and green
of earthen soil
and daily toil
and grant their blessings
from between
the thoughts and deeds
and common places
rooting into
shadow'd spaces
till hearts lift
by subtle gift
and we perceive
their hidden faces.

If ye'd plant
a spell to grow,
choose from your deck
the card to sow.
Then three above
and three below
and "bury" it that
none shall know.

As each card covers spell
to the pile this charm tell:

Say:
Sun and water nourish thee,
now from this soil, seed -
grow for me.

When all are laid,
the spell is made.
In deck conceal

that none reveal,
and thus the magic none can steal.

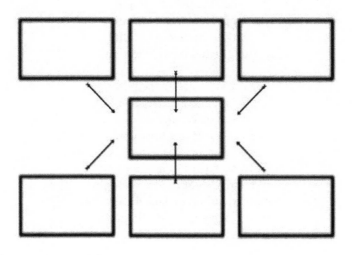

FOR VICTORY IN BATTLE

When against thy might
an opposition rears upright,
Dark be moved by Light,
as strength and confidence ignite.

Lay a card for self,
in vantage unassailable.
Lay six cards below,
at a range that is unscalable.

Turn each card to face the sky,
let them see your place on high,
then once again they face the ground,
as one by one you knock them down.

Say:
Virtue is Mine,
Power is Mine,
Wisdom is Mine,
Failure is Thine.

Then from this point on,
hold tight unto thy conviction.
If thy faith be gone,
Light departs thy contradiction.

Having seen their strength
and revealed their weakness hidden,
gaze on them at length,
and they shall do as they're bidden.

Yet remember, be ye true
and virtuous in all you do
lest Light reveal thy secrets too
and failure through disgrace ensue.

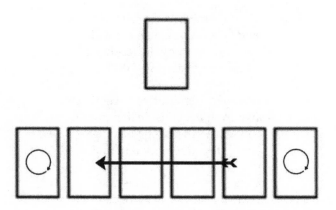

ThE FOǤ OF VISIONS

Seeing is believing,
and belief commands the will.
Let their eyes now be receiving
as their visions ye fulfill.

With thy cards, craft ye a seeming
drawn from deep inside their mind,
and set each as facet gleaming -
in this fog, they seek and find.

What they see is what is there,
whether fear or hope or care.
From within, the truth ye spin
to hang without upon the air.

In the magic they must dwell,
wrapped around with their concern
Captured deep within thy spell
until inner truth they learn.

When the fog has taught them all
and their minds no longer drift
and they've made peace with themselves
only then, the fog shall lift.

Say:
*Labyrinthine
and serpentine
to mist's design
thy sense consign.*

Yet note - if ye would make this last
the cards a mind must catch.
Let wiles hold senses, firm and fast,
lest shock undo the latch.

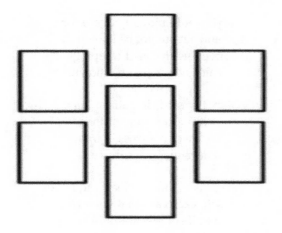

S. Rune Emerson

ᚦᚺᚲ ᛋᚺᚱᛟᚢᚲ ᛟᚠ ᚢᚾᛋᚲᚲᛁᚾᛋ
The Shroud of Unseeing

If ye would move against a foe
and act but not be known.
Wear ye this charm of weeping woe
which others fear be shown.

Lay thy cards in pattern thus,
with card inside for thee,
and over it a cross of trust
in thine own sorcery.

The cards around, a cloak and hood
with each card that you ply
a knife of fear and misery
that makes men wish to die.

Let each card but thine own remain
turned with its face to land.
Then turn thy face inside the cloak,
and thus conceal thy hand.

The cards be gathered to thy deck,
and carried close to thee,
and thus the cards keep thee concealed
from those who'd trouble be.

Say:
Knife be needle,
knife be thread
weave a veil
of death and dread.

Knot and tie
and wrap round me
and what I do
no one may see.

When ye'd return to normal state
and walk in Light once more,
lay cloaking pattern once again,
with thy card as before.

Yet turn all cards to face the Light
and once again be clear to sight.

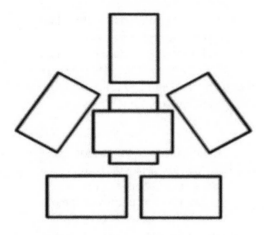

THE NORTH STAR

To know a subject utterly,
expose it to the Light
of full and clear veracity
of utter true transparency
of North Star's firm fidelity,
and ye shall know it quite.

From deck, eight cards together take
and choose and cross two there.
Around these two, a star shape make,
with one card each, its place to stake,
that truth shall shine and lies shall break
and secrets shall lay bare.

Thy crossed cards are face and mask,
the truth beneath facade.
Then one card tells you firm advice
to ward you from their fraud.
Another gives you knowledge of
the skills they do possess,
and one more card informs you how
their next move shall progress.

The last three cards are secrets -
what they think and wish revealed.
And the last card that you read,
is something they would keep concealed.

And by the laying of these cards
you've bound your subject to the Light,
and for as long as these cards lay,
their power on that one shall stay,
and whatsoe'er they do or say
must unto truth adhere outright.

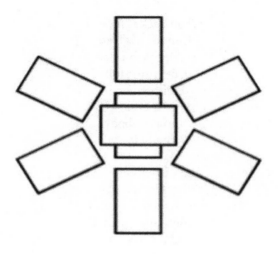

THE WINGS OF FLIGHT

When back is bowed
from heavy load
and legs are weary
from great toil.
Light as cloud
now be bestowed
upon the body
dragged to soil.

Up upon
the winds of aid
and hands so breezy
now shall hold
and carry on
to destined glade
with pacing easy
and controlled.

One card for weight
and one for thee
and for each wing
lay feathers three.

Then say the spell,
and all is well.

Say:
*Wing to work
and wind to wing -
light as air
and bright as spring!*

And spell of ease
thy woes appease.

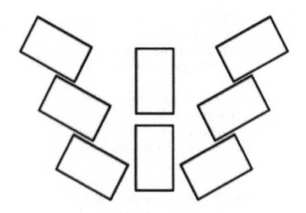

The Well of Mending

When heart and body suffer
let thy cards be remedy.
Give the Dark back to the Dark,
and let Light amend for thee.

Lay ye eight cards facing down
like the stonecraft of a well,
and turn each one's face upright,
and each card a woe shall tell.

Lay the deck inside the ring,
and let each card proclaim its tale.
Round the circle, read them all,
that the magic shall prevail.

When all cards upright do lay,
choose ye one card ye would keep.
Then the others send away
unto the pile to rest and sleep.

The remaining card is yours,
be it badge or be it scar,
and its mark upon thee be,
for wounds are part of what we are.

Take care - if nostrum ye would make
or if a tonic ye'd create,
remember pain is seen as rain -
a temporary turn of fate.

This magic has no power over
that which leaves no lasting change,
and so combine it with another
if true wellness ye'd arrange.

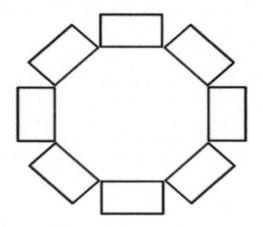

S. Rune Emerson

THE PRISON OF SHADOWS

Wicked
and deceiving
and unworthy
and untrue,

Cruel
and conniving
and unclean.

Bind them
with their sorrows
and the evil
they would do.

Bind them
in their vagaries
obscene.

One - their shadow
One - to blind
One - to catch and hold and bind

Five around to make them mind.
By their deeds are they confined.

A warning - should they pass from greed
and bravely face their evil deeds
Their loss shall be their liberty -
the shades which bind shall set them free.

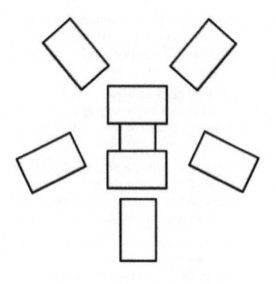

S. Rune Emerson

CHARMING THE SANCTUARY

Home and hearth are hallowed ground,
a blessing all our days.
Use this spell that place be bound
unto thy words and ways.

Lay nine cards in triquetra shape
as shown upon the page,
and speak a threefold charm for each
enchantment ye'd engage.

Each curve of cards described and laid
shall boon together give,
and joint ensorcellment is made
when knot ninefold doth live.

From each three cards, a token call -
an emblem or a sign.
And bound together each and all,
shall their nine Lights align.

And braided shall thy spell remain
and bound unto thy walls.
And blessings shall be felt and shared
by guests within thy halls.

Say:
By (name three tokens)
A thread of Light for gain.
By (three more tokens)
Another to soothe pain.
By (three last tokens)
A final thread to ward,
and by this ninefold knot
shall all attend within accord.

Yet note - thy magic wards thee well
if ye refuse a foe.
But if invited, he may dwell
unhindered to work woe.

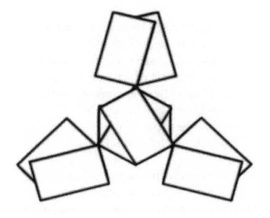

Ϯⱨε Wiϯⱨⅰⱪꞡ Wⱥll

To ward thyself from ill and harm
is never foolish toil.
A well-made ward can safely guard
from conflicts which may broil,
and blunts the weapons of a foe
and turns bewitchments fell.
Observe these pages and we'll show
just how to craft this spell.

Begin with a signification
for one who for safety yearns.
Then choose eight more in contemplation
of each danger spell now turns.

Round the subject lay the cards
in grid of nine to make a wall.
And then from each, your spell consign
a threat to stand outside them all.

Each of the eight a danger thwart,
and to thy safety lends support,
and thus thy ward shall e'er abort
all wickedness and evil sport.

Yet note, three weaknesses remain -
if any see ye weave your chain
and thus discern their purpose plain,
then they may work and craft its bane.

The card first laid is weak spot too -
if they espy its nature true,
they may attack it and cut through
thy ward, and all thy work undo.

The last weakness one can't avoid -
thy oversight can be employed.

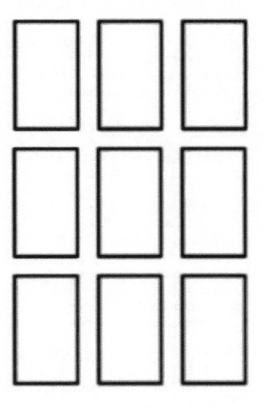

S. Rune Emerson

ThE BECKONING HAND

Mortal hearts are filled with wishes bright
as sky is filled with stars.
And since each wish possesses Light,
despair leaves burning scars.

It is no sin to seek what we
desire in our heart.
And sorcery can set Light free
to grant these with our Art.

Lay first the card to symbolize
precisely your desire.
Then round it lay four details
to define what you'd acquire.
Then lay a card beneath,
to open ways and bring it here,
and then finally a hex apply -
three cards to hold it near.

Then speak the spell and let it be,
and Light shall move the Dark,
and shadows shall reveal to thee
its coming with their mark.

Say:
Hand of joy which never tires
fly forth and do my will.
Bring me the glass of heart's desires
that I may drink my fill.

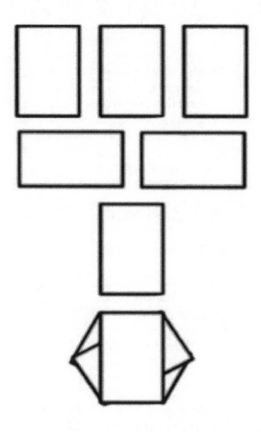

THE BALEFUL SERPENT

Lay nine cards in snake formation
to bring curse or transformation.
Say these words as each is laid,
and send them off to do as bade.

Say:
By a Bent Path,
By a Simple Path,
By a Winding Way,

Into all ye are,
Into all ye do,
Into all ye say,

Into the water,
Into the earth,
Into the air ye breathe,

I lay nine serpents
of black birth
to slither, slip, and seethe.

Name their purpose and their food,
then send them on their way.
Naught shall turn thy vengeful brood
till they have found their prey.

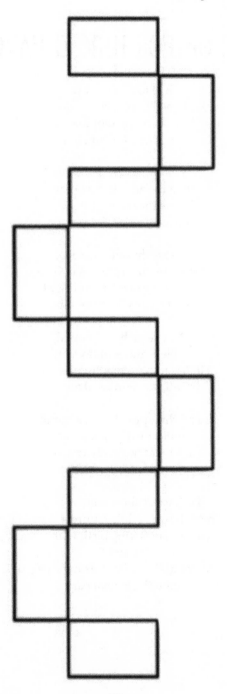

EYE OF FORTUNE'S FAVOR

Eye to counter eye,
spell to counter spell.
Use this spread of fortune,
to turn all ill and fell.

Choose a card for thee,
then round it lay six more.
These the circle of thy Art
which wards thee evermore.

Cross thyself with one,
the Light which comes to bide,
and place one left and right
to the circle's either side.

An eye ye have created,
to bless and seal thy Fate.
All threads confined to blessings,
all wickedness abate.

Read this spread once a month,
under thy chosen moon,
and that heavenly mirror
will grant to you its boon.

The Astral shows our Worth,
The Dead Unveil hearts, while nature's Wights Preserve -
The Light enchants the Divine Birth within Dark womb's
reserve.
Infernal Might assists what fortune Faery'd Serve,
upon the Primal earth.

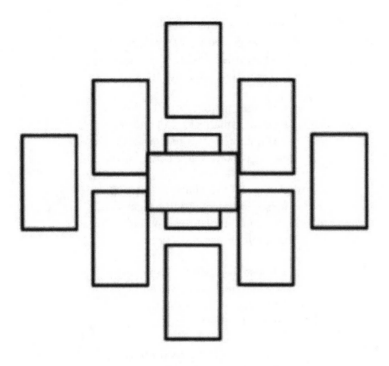

Tħe Weiȝħt'ꝺ Faꞇe

Every choice has consequences -
and every pow'r has weight.
With this spell, the Light dispenses
heaviness unto one's fate.

Used to bring about great changes
from the smallest act of choice,
Magic turns and rearranges
fate to give one's act strong voice.

Also wield this charm to burden
foes with fate's unkind regard,
to weigh them down and slow their efforts,
that their choices task them hard.

Choose the spell's significator
and lay it at point most low.
Then across it, lay their action
whereby their desires show.

Then above their head project
a line of cards of consequence.
With two above, let three cross each,
that eight show weighty subsequence.

At last, collapse each card and stack
it on their cross upon their back,
for might in haste makes burden'd fate,
and wise heads must deliberate.

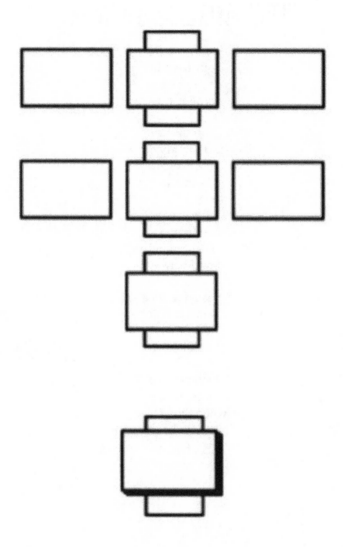

THE ENDLESS KNOT

Four from thee,
four from me,
lay thine low,
crowned be.

Cross show me
Entreaty -
pact bestow
sanctity.

Vow say thee
unto me -
quid pro quo,
bound are we.

Sealed to thee,
magic be,
virtue flow
endlessly.

Wonder be
offer'd thee
when thou show
loyalty.

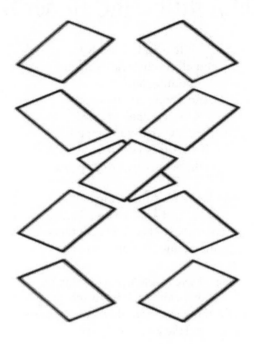

S. Rune Emerson

Sheathing the Blades

Life is full of conflict,
and all conflicts have an end.
Nothing lasts forever,
even dooms upon our head.
Use this spell to finish
a disaster beyond mend.
If all forces ye'd diminish,
set these ten cards as a spread.

Lay a card for self in battle,
and a card as thine own blade.
Then above thee lay four others,
and below four more are laid.

Up above are sharpen'd daggers,
while below each has a sheath.
Draw the knives into their counterparts
to take away their teeth.

Yet fold thine own blade also,
and uncross the sword ye wield,
and let it cover ye as armor
and convert it to a shield.

For the spell shall banish weapons,
and bring conflict to a close,
but if ye still brew contention,
then the end shall bring thee woes.
AROINT!

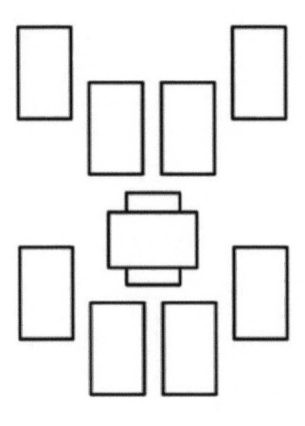

APPENDICES

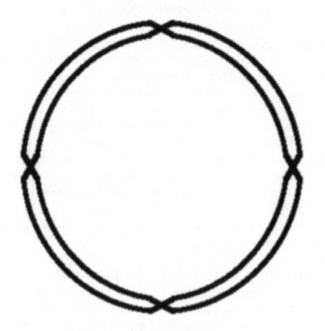

A collection of lists,
correspondences,
and notations,
which will hopefully
assist the reader
in further study
and practical development

Remedies and Ritual Tokens

Some acts of magic aren't actually spells, nor are they rituals. Simple acts of sorcery, such as blessing water or magicking a candle with a blessing spell, are minor charms which can have a very potent effect when done correctly. Seemingly small, these little things can nevertheless pack a wallop.

Tokens, for example, are extremely effective ways to banish dangerous spirits, and also can be helpful in making offerings to good spirits as well. Indeed, much of what people view as ceremonial magic in Eastern tradition is merely the act of offering honor and grace to a spirit or group of spirits, so as to create a purified space. And of course, astrological magicians created "tilsam," which is the root of the word "talisman" we use nowadays - an Image which creates a change upon the world in a favorable way. The most common of these were simple luck charms, blessed by the light of a combination of planets in a favorable aspect.

Tokens are the currency of the magical world. Spirits enjoy anything beautiful or virtuous - the scent of good incense, an offering of pure water or wine, a paper charm or brightly ribboned decoration, etc. Usually these offerings are given with the spirit and its lore in mind; a nature spirit such as a flower nymph may be well-pleased when one offers good water to a beautiful flower, or otherwise helps nature. A blessed house spirit (like a fenodyree or brownie) may often be partial to certain offerings of food - for example, milk and honey and buttered bread. They are pleased by that which pleases a child, but only the healthiest and most reverent of offerings are truly honored.

A magician practicing Cartomantic Sorcery can use cards as her tokens, or she can choose her tokens from some part of the cards she works with. A wielder of a deck rife with Celtic knot-work might tie knots or draw a knot-work emblem on a card as a gift to the spirits. Many professional readers who work magic build spells into their business cards, so they can double as offerings when they cast spells. And, of course, magic is never amiss as an offering to spirits. One can do a divination or a fate-bending to bring fortune to the spirit's locus, if one is visiting and seeks to maintain goodwill.

In addition, a magician must remember that all his offerings must reflect his nature, his magic, and what he finds sacred, alongside the kinship of the spirit. Remember that a relationship moves the world; offerings are a way of relating to the spirits. In any case, a few things are always necessary for a Cartomantic Sorcerer who works with a spirit:

A small container of strewing material - a cartomancer will likely create a dust from the ash of a card or cartomantic sigil, and perhaps combine it with salt or glitter or herbs, so as to be able to use it for marking as well as casting. This dust can be used to offer a blessing over something, to draw the Umbra of one's deck over something, and also to ward against ill spirits, usually by marking a subject with it. Mixing it with crushed herbs and resins can also allow it to be a good incense to burn, if that is the wont of the magician.

A bell - often used to ring a blessing into a space from the cards. Placing the bell atop a card, and then whispering its name or secret into the mouth of the bell and ringing it can set a circle and offer forth its magic as a power into a space.

A collection of coins or material tokens (I use silver keys, for example) to give as gifts. Ribbons, charms, and colored beads are also traditional; using cords can also allow one to tie a knot of magic into a gift, which makes them valuable in more ways than one.

To bless something within the embrace of your Cartomancy, simply lay your tokens upon your reading cloth and say a prayer of honor over it, something like this:

By the Light which shapes the Dark
By the Dark which holds the Light
In the Embrace of the Vision, the Signs, and the Spirits,
I bless these goodly things that they may walk in Triumph.

The thing about prayer is, it must be genuinely from the heart and honest. Unlike spells, which are essentially a borrowed or harnessed reflection of the outside world, a prayer is a reflection of one's own self and being. Therefore, it cannot be artificial. Be sure to use no one else's words but your own, and be honest and true as you speak to your idea of the divine.

S. Rune Emerson

To offer something to the spirits, do the following: cleanse and wash yourself, wear clean clothes if possible, and then go to the place where they dwell. Lay your cards out in a circle which you have created, and place the token you have for them within it, and then bow your head in mutual respect. Speak as if they can hear you. If you cannot sense them, that may mean they are concealing themselves from you. Say what is true in your heart, and do not lie. Tell them why you have come, and what you bring them. A pure heart is a star of Fortune; it shines and inspires. If the spirits decide to help you, then that is up to them. If they do not, well... making offering to the spirits is always a good idea, even if they don't grant your wish. It helps cleanse the spirit, and helps one restore balance and harmony.

In addition to the various tokens one can offer, there are also magical forms of medicine that a bit of sorcery can aid. When blending medicines or remedies from herbs and ingredients, always remember that the nostrum being crafted must reflect the world and its nature:

One set of ingredients shall be the Noon, offering the warmth of its spirit as the strength of the remedy - this is usually the dominant or "tonic" herb.

One set of ingredients shall be the Dusk, reflecting the inner mystery and subtle power of the remedy - this is usually a supplemental or subtle herb.

One set of ingredients shall be the Dawn, holding the true message and purpose of the remedy - this is usually the definitive herb, whose property is most needed.

The last ingredient shall be the Night, the medium in which the remedy is concocted, such as alcohol or water, or in the case of incense, resin or tree-bark.

Each ingredient (or set of ingredients) will be blended separately and enchanted in a manner that is chosen by one's tarot cards. If a spell calls for cinnamon, and one draws the Two of Cups, let that cinnamon be a gift blessed by two hearts which love each other. This allows one to blend one's cartomancy with the mixing of remedies, strengthening the Light within them and making them into a truly potent elixir.

The Remedy Spread

To create such a remedy (or indeed, any simple sort of spell not strictly needing the application of Cartomantic Sorcery), one may apply a spread which teaches how to craft spells. This is a variation on a popular spread I created years ago, called the Grimoire Spread. In this version, it is specifically tailored to the crafting of remedies and simple incantations within the tradition of Cartomantic Sorcery (although perhaps without the higher aspects of the Practices being involved).

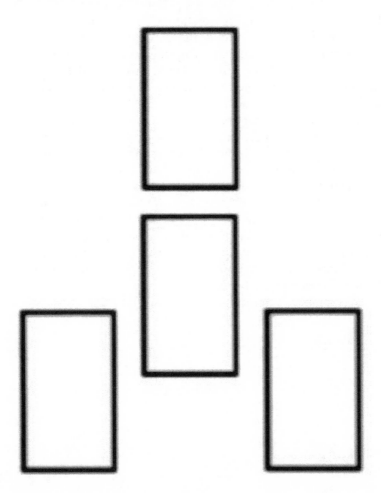

The card in the center is the Night ingredient, representing the conducting Medium of one's spell. Perhaps the Ace of Cups might come up here to let us know that we must brew a potion, or the Eight of Swords will imply that one must gather ground water or rust (swords planted in water tend to rust) as the primary component.

The bottom right card is the Noon ingredient, depicting the Medium of main power for the spell. The Six of Coins might suggest generosity as being necessary for all ingredients collected, or an incantation being based on gifts. Perhaps the Justice card might require the weighing of one's ingredients on a scale first before adding them to a potion, whereas the Wheel of Fortune might require coins won through a game of chance.

The bottom left card is the Dusk ingredient, which of course brings in the secondary magic of the spell, to reinforce it. An incantation with the Four of Wands card here might suggest that the spell will require cooperation of others as you cast it, so perhaps weave an element of cooperation and assistance from natural spirits into your spell. A potion ingredient chosen from the Empress card might be a flower or fruit, which is meant to sustain the imbiber while the other components do their work.

The top card is the Dawn ingredient, acting as the purpose and manifestation of the spell. This focuses the goal and expresses the desired change. A Seven of Cups card might induce confusion, whereas a Two of Wands might bring foresight. Ingredients might include a crystal added to a charm object which possesses the power of the Hermit to bring wisdom in dark places, or ground nutmeg taken from a wealthy house to bring the wealth of the Ten of Coins.

A sample remedy might include the following:

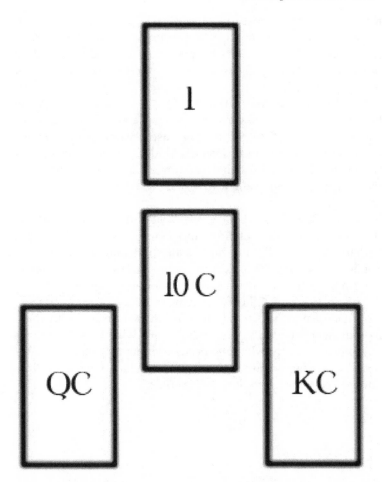

Clearly, here we have a remedy known as a Philtre - a bewitchment potion, commonly referred to as a love potion. Now, as most of the cards here (especially the Ten of Cups in the center) are cards based around water or cups, I will say that this requires either water or wine. However, whatever it is mixed in must be in a place of happiness and hope, as befits the Ten of Cups. The Night ingredient in this instance will not be the water, but rather the vessel from which the potion is drunk.

The Noon ingredient is the King of Cups, and that suggests water again, but as this ingredient is intended to draw strength to the potion, perhaps a liquor or beverage given by a man who evokes those qualities which the King of Cups is known for. The King of Cups is also known as the Fisher King (yes, from the Grail mythos). So, perhaps gather the water from a nearby river, or maybe use an already present liquor used for healing and medicine.

The Dusk ingredient is the Queen of Cups, once again bringing water into the story, this time as a vessel of confidence and heart's ease. One could easily use a calming herb in the brew, such as chamomile. One could also gather water upon a flat silver mirror, and use that as a subtle ingredient of reflection. Or, perhaps stir the water with a stalk of willow, and murmur a secret into it.

The Dawn ingredient is the Magician, which acts as the final ingredient (that of love and bewitchment in this case). Perhaps the roses of life and death (red and white) can be applied, scattering the petals upon the surface of the water in one's mixing bowl, and whispering one's spell over it, or letting them rest under the light of Dawn for an hour.

One could also brew an infusion of rose tea with these ingredients fairly easily, and adding some willow or chamomile might make exactly what one needs to bring a philtre to perfect potency. Mixing an infusion of rose and chamomile or willow into mulled wine may not be amiss either.

RITUAL MAGIC CONTRACTS

A Contract is a powerful thing, especially to a sorcerer. For some sorcerers, Contracts with spirits are at the core and heart of much of their magic. To truly harness the power of sorcery, one must remember that a sorcerer is still a sorcerer even if she has no tools, no spirits, and no tokens. That being said, Contracts are key to further developing oneself as a magician; they are in fact one of the six paths of Initiation, as we discussed in an earlier part of this book.

For a sorcerer, there are three really important kinds of Contracts one may enter into:

A Familiar-type Contract such as was previously mentioned in the Book of Counted Images or the relationship created between one and one's tools.

A Contract with a client wherein both parties gain and sacrifice accordingly.

A Contract of Patronage from a guiding force or spirit, such as the one created when one uses the Fool's Journey and chooses a Guide from the Trumps.

Now, as much as a sorcerer is a sorcerer with or without her tools, some kinds of magic cannot be accomplished alone. Occasionally, one's own wisdom is not enough to accommodate a particular spell, or one might need some reinforcement of strength from an aligned source. These are the common reasons magicians create Pacts with greater spirits who act as Patrons to the magician, providing guidance and training in one's Arte, and also lending strength and benefit to the practitioner in exchange for service.

If one would seek to petition a Patron with a Contract:

Step One - bring an offering and enter your Magic Circle.

Step Two - make your request and lay down your offering, along with the Contract to be held.

Step Three - wait for a sign or visitation from the spirit in question.

If you receive no sign, you may perform divination to see if they have accepted the offer. It is not unheard of to have a spirit wait and see how a person will react to a seeming lack of response; occasionally the Ordeal of a spirit Contract comes in the form of a test from the spirit. That being said, persistence and earnest clarity of heart are the best method by which one can approach a Contract.

In truth, some spirits are simply harder to interact with peacefully. Sorcery was built upon the principle of working with the spiritual and the Unseen, and our natural gifts allow us to do this without any aid. If you have difficulty getting the attention of a particular spirit, try the following:

Challenge it to a contest, and accept the terms of its test.

Offer it an offering of service rather than an object.

Commune with it and express your reason for needing help.

Perform a blessing and a divination for it, as a gift without request for service.

Once you have made your offering, allow the spirit the ability to respond. If you are not in harmony with the spirit, you will likely not understand its message, and it may not even be able to help you. Continue to connect to it without regard for reward, in the ways we discussed above. This will create an affinity between you and the spirit you are seeking to bond with. If you feel you are unable to connect to the spirit or force, you can always choose something else to bond with; do not be discouraged. Use your will and be determined. Spirits respond to your diligence and Strength.

A cartomancer's primary Contracts (referred to here as Pacts) are most likely to be with the Patrons of their deck. In our particular brand of Cartomantic Sorcery, there are six obvious potential Patrons one can easily form a Contract with. These are the six Trumps which represents the Lights of Initiation: the Magician, the High Priestess, the Empress, the Emperor, the Lovers, and Temperance. However, any of the Trumps (or Courts for that matter) within a deck might suit one as a Patron. For that matter, one might prefer not one Patron but all six, or maybe even all twenty-two of the Trumps or what have you.

In any case, a Pact of Patronage usually involves the following: the magician swears to some sort of behavior or action, which they will regularly uphold, and in exchange they will receive powers and privileges from their Patron. An example might include an oath to the High Priestess to speak only truth and answer any question when asked, which allows one to see the future and know the hidden. Or, perhaps a promise to hold a monthly rite in honor of the Magician, and thereby gain the ability to call upon spirits of Infernal power simply by making his gesture.

It is by these methods and many others that a sorcerer will learn the greater Artes of moving Light. For this reason, a great many cartomantic magicians learn secret languages and ciphers and sigilic symbol-systems which allow them the ability to reference their Cards quickly and surreptitiously. Qabalists will learn Hebrew to reference the Trumps via incantation, whereas an astrologer might learn the planetary associations and astrological correspondences with the various cards so as to cast simple spells via symbolic gesture or word.

The accessing of one's Pacts through simple symbolism is a standard practice for magicians of all kinds - and the forming of such things is a standard practice amongst all kinds of magical practitioners. Whether one calls upon gods one worships in possessory invocation, or speaks a spell naming places one has encountered via astral travel, these spells are not so much spells as thaumaturgic triggers for an already present act of theurgy. Speaking secret Names, using arcane gestures of significance, singing a particular verse sacred to one's Patron ... these are methods of using the Cards without having them present. This method is also employed when calling upon spirit-Familiars or any other Contracted force - a true spell or working has already been performed, and one is simply calling upon it where it is needed.

For example, a simple method of incantation to call upon the powers of the Magic Circle would call upon the three areas within it:

Upon the Path of (speak code-word for one of the four Path Trumps)
I greet the Light of (speak code-word for one of the six Initiation Trumps)
Yield unto me the Rays of (desired Art)
By (describe the Trump associated with the Art)

Ex:
Upon the Path of the Hanged Man
I greet the Light of the Priestess.

Yield unto me the Rays of Knowing
By the distant Lamp of the hidden Hermit.

Feel free to use this as inspiration to make your own format of incantation, as it is merely meant to be an example of card-less incantation.

REGARDING GROUP WORK AND THE COURT

Sorcerers are ordinarily rather solitary creatures, practicing and learning their Art in private, inviting others into the Adytum of their Magic Circle sparingly, and taking on students only when philosophy and physical vitality shift their thoughts toward legacy. Their need for companionship usually comes from their more mortal concerns, and often has little to do with their magic. However, it is for this very reason (and many others besides) that a sorcerer may find their lives enriched by working in concert with other magicians of goodly nature and intent.

As a sorcerer's solitary nature is bent toward sovereignty over their sphere of influence, it behooves them to be wary when accepting invitations into ritual circles or lodges, as the structure of hierarchy imposed upon a sorcerer by others is tantamount to an attack or act of oppression upon a sorcerer's nature and magical Will. Therefore, it is best when one's efforts in a group of magicians are joined only where none lead or hold sway, but rather all are bent upon cooperative action toward mutual goals.

The following is a small guide one may use to create a magical group based upon Cartomantic Sorcery and Tarot. In order to avoid association with witches' covens and hierarchical lodges of high magic, we shall name our style of group after the conventions of the Tarot itself. A magical group of practitioners of this brand of Cartomantic Sorcery is called a Court, and each Court has its own title or epithet linking it to the common kind(s) of magic practiced by its members. A Court which primarily practices subtly and is strong in secrecy might call themselves the Unseen Court, or perhaps more floridly the Court of Shadows. A Court which functioned in allegiance to a particular deity (the god Hermes for example) might call themselves something in alignment with its principles (the Court of Winged Heels for example).

In any case, once a Court has its name and vision, mutually agreed upon, it is recommended that they develop a visual standard, a heraldic sigil or banner which acts as the Image of the Court's work. The Unseen Court might draw an eye behind a veil, while the Court of Winged Heels might have a depiction of a winged heel as their sigil. Whatever Image they choose, it should be applied in nearly every formal or official act the Court finds themselves engaged in. The name of a Court, and its sigil, operate as the Sword and Wand of the group, defining and warding the power they raise, and also enacting talismanic change upon those who encounter the powers associated with the Court (members and uninitiated alike).

From this point, a Court may engage in the raising up of an Adytum from the circle of their shared Light. This is of course done by choosing a Tarot deck through which the combined magicks of the Court shall be worked. The deck chosen should be selected carefully, so as to conduct Light properly in adherence to the vision of the Court. This deck shall act as the Coin of the Court, the embodied Corpus of magic and strength of each sorcerer's enlisted Light, either borne forth directly from their own soul or entwined via Contracts. An Adytum is an elevated altar comprised of and dedicated to the Light which moves the Dark. In Cartomantic Sorcery, the Adytum is comprised of the 22 Trumps of the Tarot, representing the manifold Lights of the universe in all their various forms. This is why the Magic Circle spread is created entirely from the Trumps, as we have examined in previous areas in this book.

Once the deck has been chosen upon which to build the Adytum of the Court, each member shall choose a single Trump to act as their Patron while within the Court's Umbra. These Patrons are the Grail through which the Light of the Court's Adytum shall enter each member's life, empowering and shaping the Darkness around them through its signs and endowments. One who chooses the Lovers, for example, may find potency in fruit and fire (emblems of the Lovers' power), and may also find themselves developing a harmony with the Light of Resonance.

In any case, this choosing should come hand in hand with an Oath, as the binding of Light through Contract is the surest way to create a proper Medium of one's relationship to a Patron. A sample Oath will be included in this chapter, but essentially the Oath sworn to the Patron must convey the following: a promise to follow the tenets of the sorcerer's nature, an oath of loyalty to the powers of magic (the Light and the Dark), and a pact of alliance, peace, and privacy between all members of the Court. Each Contract witnessed under the Patron (who for each of us is the administrator of the Light of the Adytum) shall convey a benefit in exchange for adherence. As we are loyal to ourselves, so the Patron rewards our endeavors with guidance; as we serve the Light, so the Patron will ensure that the Light will serve us faithfully and never forsake us; as we serve our allies, so shall the Patron ensure that we are defended from trouble at the hands of the other sorcerers. That oath of peace and mutual respect alone is enough to justify the creation of a Pact in an area wherein there are a large number of sorcerers with conflicting agendas.

Once the bond is made, the Trumps should be gathered together, and a calendar should be laid in the following pattern:

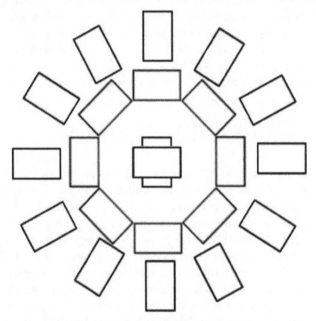

This spread is known as the Oraculum, and it depicts the following:

Twelve moons (with the thirteenth in the center as the crossing card), which act as monthly workings and rites to be held.

Eight high holy days (distributed roughly equidistantly

across the year), which denote times for acts of offering and sacrifice.

An Overseer of the entire Court for the year (the innermost card), who facilitates the goals and interests of the Court otherwise.

This Oraculum shall be used as a prediction of the year's events and tides, and also shall give assignment to the Court for works to be done and magicks to be learned.

REGARDING THE HOLY DAYS

It is traditional to use holidays which are significant to the members of the Court. A Court which has ties to European paganism or Wicca might feel inclined towards using the modern Wheel of the Year innovated from the ancient sabbats of pagan worship. A strongly Greek-influenced Court might use the holy days of different gods, while Roman-influenced sorcerers might apply holidays such as Saturnalia and Lupercalia to their work. However the days are chosen, it is recommended that they be roughly six weeks apart, so as not to overtax the Court's resources.

REGARDING THE MOONS

The working of magic in harmony with the phases of the Moon is a traditional practice for many schools of magic, ancient and modern alike. That being said, which phase of the Moon one performs one's working upon may change based on a number of factors. If there are thirteen full moons in the year, one might select to simply schedule the calendar in adherence with the full moons (with the thirteenth moon rite being held upon the extra moon in a month or the third in a season of four - the tradition of the "blue moon"). However, if there are thirteen new moons and only twelve full moons, a Court might elect to utilize the dark moons instead of the full (with the thirteenth "black moon" being accessed in a similar manner to the "blue moon"). Still other Courts may choose to utilize the actual phases of the moon, scheduling their rites in accordance with the principles of waxing and waning. It all depends on the Court's practice and mutual vision.

Regarding The Overseer

It is understood that disputes will happen in a group full of powerful wills. The yearly Overseer is chosen to remove authority from the hands of any individual, and instead place it in the hands of the Light itself, which is truly how any sorcerer should view their magical philosophy anyway. The Light empowers us, the Dark rewards us, and so we serve them loyally.

Any conflict of interest which arises within a Court should always be resolved by discussion and mutual agreement if at all possible, but if this proves an ineffective approach, then the conflict should be resolved through consultation of the Patron through the cards. If the Patron chosen as Overseer for the year is the personal Patron of one of the members, then they shall be the ones who consult and find the solution. If the Overseer is no member's Patron (after all, each member should have an individual Patron unless the number of the Court's members exceeds 22), then the reader shall be chosen by high card (all who wish to read shall draw a card, and the high card wins). However one arrives at one's chosen reader, that reader will read the cards under the auspices of the Overseer, and shall lay cards to reveal solutions to conflict, rather than to engender conflict or to promote dispute. For example, if two people have conflicting ideas on how to enact a monthly rite, the cards will be consulted for the Overseer's suggestion on how the rite should be conducted, and the cards shall not be asked which of the members is "right."

Should a direct conflict erupt between two or more members in the Court, the cards shall once again be consulted, this time to decide how to resolve the conflict. For example, if three sorcerers all seek to cast conflicting spells upon a shared workplace, the cards shall act as final judgment on what works shall be enacted over the locale in question, and the three disputing sorcerers shall be expected to each work toward that end in concert.

In the end, this takes all sense of injustice or offense away from members of the Court, and reminds each member of their loyalty to the Light and what it reveals.

ENTERING THE COURT: AN INITIATION RITE

You will need:

• *A chalice or bowl of water, wine, or other representation of the Cup, with a method of asperging or sprinkling said liquid.*
• *A wand or other representation of the Rod*
• *A bladed weapon or other representation of the Sword*
• *A bowl of coins, salt, or other representation of the currency of the Coin*
• *A cloth or working surface for your rite, which should act as a tarot cloth and also an altar space - you can elevate it upon a table, or lay it upon the ground as you choose*
• *The tarot deck used to create the Adytum of the Court*
• *The book associated with the Court's magical lore*
• *Any appropriate ritual implements used by personal traditions of the Court's members: incense, candles, etc. A unique source of light should be used, although the precise form is up to the ritual participants.*

Note: this Rite is a dedication ritual for the convening and entering of a Court. Each verse in the dedication can be spoken by a different attending member. In the event one finds oneself to be more experienced than those others seeking admission to one's magical group (and therefore one is planning on creating one's own Court and inviting members to attend later), one can speak all parts individually, and merely use the last part of this Rite for others to participate in, which means the setting of space and laying of the Adytum spread shall be up to the creator of the Court, who shall henceforth be known as the Initiator.

PREPARING THE RITE

Begin by cleansing the space in whatever fashion is most appropriate to you. Burn incense, light candles, play music, and perform any personal cleansing rites you choose to perform. Stand in the center of your work place, and take up the Sword, speaking the following spell:

> *Word and blade, now draw the line*
> *of truth, of Knowledge and of Care.*
> *Bind Infernal and Divine,*
> *to consecrate against despair.*
> *Tween perfect Light and fertile Darkness,*
> *these confines I give to Need.*
> *Blessed against profane in every form -*
> *in thought, in word, indeed*

Return the blade to the altar, and take up the Cup. Walk the circle clockwise again, sprinkling water along the way. Speak these words:

> *Redden, ground, with blood of Art.*
> *Charm the space and bless the Heart.*
> *Courage rise, from Mirror'd sea -*
> *We become the Mystery.*

Return the chalice to the altar, and then pick up the Rod, and point first at the East, then South, then West, then North, repeating this incantation at each:

> *Gates of Image and design,*
> *Open wide and thus align.*
> *From these portals, pow'r instill -*
> *All in service to our Will.*

Point the wand at the altar, and speak firmly:

> *By Arcana's open door*
> *Might is wakened evermore.*

Return the wand to the altar, and take up the Coin. Walk the circle deosil a final time, and scatter a pinch/coin in the eight compass directions as you walk. Incant this verse:

> *Salt be salt, and gold be gold.*
> *All in Silence, truth is told.*
> *Cards of bounty, cards of Fate.*
> *Here thy Body we create.*

Finish your preparations with the following affirmation:

> *The Shadows are cast and thus remain,*
> *Across time and space, in every plane.*

LAYING THE ADYTUM

Separate your Trumps into the Circle of the Adytum, and speak the incantations as you go.

Create first the Compass:

> *In Commitment to Knowledge and with Mighty Will,*
> *Nurturing all Courage with Virtuous Silence,*
> *we walk with the Light which moves the Dark.*

Next, make the Talisman:

> *By the Six Lights of Initiation,*
> *the Game begins.*

Finally, craft the Circle thus:

> *Let the Lights of Art surround us,*
> *in the Adytum of this Court.*
> *May we Walk in Triumph.*

ADMISSION TO THE COURT

Seekers of entry into the Court shall now step forward, one by one. Each shall choose one of the cards to be turned, and that shall reveal their Patron. Under its auspices, the Challenge shall be issued:

> *By what name do you come here?*
> *(seeker gives their sorcerer's name)*

> *Why seek you this Court?*
> *(await their answer)*

> *Come you here of your own free will?*
> *(await their answer)*

> *Choose then, a Patron who shall sponsor you.*
> *(allow them to choose from the Adytum spread)*

When the Patron is selected, the Oath is given:

First, the Covenant of the Compass:
(name of seeker)
Do you swear to adhere to the principles of the Sorcerer's Art
ever striving to uphold Commitment to Knowledge,
maintaining a Mighty Will,
Courageously endeavoring to Nurture,
and keeping all in Virtuous Silence
to the best of your ability?
(await answer)

Second, the Covenant of the Talisman:
Do you promise yourself henceforth
to the Light which moves
and the Dark which is shaped,
forsaking all others who would hinder this loyalty?
(await answer)

Finally, the Covenant of the Circle:
Do you swear to offer no harm
to any bound to this Court,
and to keep hidden any ways,
arts, or secrets learned herein
from any not initiated,
save when given express permission to do otherwise?
(await answer)

When all answers are given in the affirmative, the Oath is witnessed. Have the seeker sign the back of the book and draw their sigil if they have one.

Once all seekers are dedicated, the Oraculum may be held, and the year shall be prophesied. The Rite is finished, and the Court is gathered. Any further Court business can be taken up at this time.

This ritual should be enacted but once a year, so as to allow the members to learn well each other's ways and nature.

May you walk in Triumph!

ThE GAME OF TRIUMPh

One of the rituals of Tarot magic relies upon the fact that the cards are essentially a game, and can be played as such as a magical game. For the Court, there is a very simple method of playing which one can employ. It is reminiscent of Crazy 8's, and we will describe it thus.

Players: optimally between 3 and 6 (although can accommodate 2 players and a full deck can accommodate up to 8 players)

Goal: to be the first to discard all cards from one's hand.

Players each draw a hand of seven cards from the deck. The top card of the remainder is turned over by whoever last shuffled. If a Trump is shown, the suit is chosen - otherwise, play as normal. This card is the significator of the spell - the subject upon whom the magic of the Court is to be focused. The person who deals this top card (called the dealer) will determine who or what the spell is focused upon, and what the goal is.

Players (beginning with the person to the left of the dealer, going clockwise) will each play to the pile created by the significator. Each card must match either suit or numeric value. If one has no match, one can play a Trump and choose a suit (but smaller Trumps can only be beaten by larger ones or the Fool, and the Fool can be beaten by any other Trump). If one has no playable card, a player may draw once from the draw pile (the remainder of face-down cards). If that card is not playable, they pass their turn.

However, this isn't merely a game - it's a ritual as well. Players are altering the circumstances and fate of the subject, moving it toward the goal chosen by the dealer. As such, each card played must be spoken into effect as a spell. One might play the Three of Coins while trying to affect the subject (originally the Lovers, which the dealer decided was a newlywed couple having a rocky time), granting the gift of a marvelous day at work where one's efforts are appreciated and praised. That could easily be a step toward the goal, but of course that card is easily bent in the direction of good fortune. The real challenge comes when one seeks to spend a card like the Ten of Swords to further such a kindly goal.

This kind of game employs one's creative imagination and vision, as well as one's Will and ability to surrender to the cards.

When one finally has one card left in their hand, one must speak the word "Triumph" as they play their second-to-last card. If they are caught by the others having forgotten such an action, they must draw three more. If they play one more round and lay their last card, they win. Remember the final goal of the spell, and make sure to tie it up nicely.

When the draw pile is gone, the significator pile (the face up cards) is shuffled and placed once more in the draw pile, and play resumes until someone wins.

H MAP TO THE COUNTED IMAGES

Aid and Healing
Calling of the Jack, Induce a Humor, Petition Winter, Conjure Rain, Turn the Winds, Travel in Safety, Wings of Flight, Well of Mending, Charming the Sanctuary, Beckoning Hand, Baleful Serpent, Eye of Fortune's Favor, Endless Knot, Sheathing the Blades

Fortune and Gain
Calling of the Jack, Scales of Gain, Draw Wayward Souls, Plant a Seed, Beckoning Hand, Eye of Fortune's Favor
Insight and Understanding
Knight's Vigil, Queen's Mirror, Conjure an Omen, Commune With Another, Cause Reflection, Conjure Rain, Fog of Visions, North Star, Well of Mending, Weight'd Fate

Luck and Success
Calling of the Jack, Conjure an Omen, Ensure an Advantage, Open the Way, Turn the Winds, Red Carpet, Plant a Seed, Victory in Battle, Wings of Flight, Eye of Fortune's Favor, Weight'd Fate, Endless Knot

Knowledge and Information
Knight's Vigil, Queen's Mirror, Conjure an Omen, See from Afar, North Star, Eye of Fortune's Favor

Persuasion and Influence
Magic Circle, Calling of the Jack, Persuasion and Influence, Bespeak a Heart, Ensure an Advantage, Induce a Humor, Send a Message, Brew a Tempest, Red Carpet, Draw Wayward Souls, Victory in Battle, North Star, Charming the Sanctuary, Baleful Serpent

Protection and Safety
Magic Circle, Knight's Vigil, Conceal a Secret, Sequester Beyond Time, Ward Repose, Brew a Tempest, Travel in Safety, Victory in Battle, Fog of Visions, Shroud of Unseeing, Charming the Sanctuary, Witching Wall, Eye of Fortune's Favor, Sheathing the

Blades
Vengeance and Harm
Calling of the Jack, Send a Message, Brew a Tempest, Prison of Shadows, Baleful Serpent, Weight'd Fate

Virtue and Adepthood
Magic Circle, Making of Spells, Queen's Mirror, Bless a Bond, Plant a Seed, Fog of Visions, Endless Knot

REFERENCES

[1] "Episode 1x17- Hat Trick." *Once Upon a Time*. ABC. March 25 2012. Television

[2] R. Steele." A notice of the Ludus Triumphorum and Some Early Italian Card Games: With Some Remarks on the Origin of the Game of Cards," Archaeologia, vol LVII, 1900. pp. 185–200

[3] Antoine Court de Gébelin. *Le Monde primitif, analysé et comparé avec le monde moderne* ("The Primeval World, Analyzed and Compared to the Modern World"), volume viii. 1781

[4] Peter Carroll. *Liber Kaos*, pp. 75

[5] Herman Slater and Ed Buczynski. *Earth Religion News*. 1973-1976

FURTHER READING

A Gathering of Masks, Robert Fitzgerald, Three Hands Press, 2010 (an excellent book on tarot as a theurgical series of rites)

Azoetia: a Grimoire of the Sabbatic Craft, Andrew Chumbley, Xoanon, 1992 (probably the best text available for learning sorcery)

The Devil's Picture Book, Paul Huson, Sphere Books Ltd, 1971 (a classic book by a well-known occultist and very handy for learning the tarot from a magical perspective)

Lux Haeresis: The Light Heretical, Daniel Schulke, Xoanon Publications, 2011 (for furthering one's development in the paradigm of Light and Dark)

Mystical Origins of the Tarot, Paul Huson, Destiny Books, 2004 (more interesting and in-depth information regarding tarot and magic)

The Picatrix: Liber Rubeus Edition, John Michael Greer, Renaissance Astrology & Adocentyn Press, 2011 (primarily useful when learning the Light paradigm, and also the origin of images and talismanic sorcery)

Tarot and Magic, Donald Michael Kraig, Llewellyn Publications, 2003 (innovative, and thought-provoking when tying the sacred to the practical)

Tarot Spells, Janina Renee, Llewellyn Publications, 1990 (a fun read, and one of the first books in the modern market on the subject of tarot magic)

AUTHOR BIO

S. Rune Emerson has been a practicing witch and magician since the early 90's, and is the founder of the Risting Tradition of American Witchcraft, a tradition centered around the practice of witchcraft as a profession or skill, rather than a religious practice. He specializes in divination (especially cartomancy), and has terribly romantic notions about magic as an art-form. He spends his time singing, writing magical prose, and spying on people via his tarot cards, which are especially nosy.

GET MORE AT IMMANION PRESS

Visit us online to browse our books, sign-up for our e-newsletter and find out about upcoming events for our authors, as well as interviews with them. Visit us at http://www.immanion-press.com and visit our publicity blog at

http://ipmbblog.wordpress.com/

GET SOCIAL WITH IMMANION PRESS

Find us on Facebook at
http://www.facebook.com/immanionpress

Follow us on Twitter at
http://www.twitter.com/immanionpress
Find us on Google Plus at
https://plus.google.com/u/0/b/104674738262224210355/

CPSIA information can be obtained
at www.ICGtesting.com
Printed in the USA
BVHW031817090819
555523BV00003B/501/P

9 780993 237195